# THE CORNISH CAPTAIN'S TALE

Admiral Nelson's "band of brothers", those notable fighting captains of the Napoleonic Wars, have been amply described in biography and fiction. Here we have the life story of a Cornish sea officer of the previous generation, one who showed no less courage and devotion to duty. Richard Spry fought in campaigns which carried him from the Mediterranean to the West Indies, from the tropical heat of India, to the frozen coasts of North America. His career had its share of fortune and misfortune, but he survived to become Rear Admiral Sir Richard Spry, and to die at home in his beloved Cornwall.

Laurence O'Toole is well qualified to write this tale. He has been to sea in square rigged sailing ships, served in the wartime navy, and is familiar with many of the coasts which form the background of Richard Spry's story.

*Captain R. Spry R.N. c. 1750*

# THE CORNISH CAPTAIN'S TALE

Laurence O'Toole

Illustrated by Kingsley Cruise

**DYLLANSOW TRURAN**

Published by Dyllansow Truran
Trewolsta, Trewirgie, Redruth, Cornwall

© 1986 L. O'Toole

Printed and bound in Great Britain
by A. Wheaton & Co. Ltd, Exeter

ISBN 1 85022 011 5

# CONTENTS

# CHAPTER I

## THE FIGHT OFF NANTUCKET SHOAL

Captain Richard Spry R.N., master and commander of the bomb-sloop "Comet",[1] sat in his dim diminutive cabin, contemplating the tip of his quill-pen, and the task before him. It was not an unpleasant duty, on this occasion, but he would rather have been doing it at some other time.

The air in the cabin was damp and stuffy, for the stern windows were closely sealed against the freezing cold of the New England winter. From the deck close above his head he could hear bumps, and the sound of dragging, signifying the removal of the ship's swivel guns. Similar but heavier noises came from beyond the doorway which led through the bulkhead on to the main deck. Above the rumbling he could hear the uplifted voices of the "Comet's" gunner and Lieutenant Bridges who together were directing the landing of the six pounder carriage guns. Nearly every man of the ship's company was engaged in unloading her heavy equipment; guns, shot, powder, sails, anchors, beer barrels and water breakers were all being swung over the side on to the quay. For at high tide tomorrow the "Comet" must be floated on to the repair slip, and it would be necessary to get her as high up the ways as possible.

Captain Spry would have preferred to have been out on deck himself, seeing that everything was being done properly. He had held command of the sloop for little more than a month and he still found it hard to cultivate the remoteness expected of a captain. Besides he was deeply interested in the mechanics of shifting heavy weights with blocks and tackles. However, his years spent as a lieutenant had told him that on most occasions it was better if the captain kept out of the way, and left such matters to the ship's officers.

Besides, there was this business of the letter which had to be written at once. He had been told only an hour before that there was a naval brig, bound for Antigua in the morning. She would carry despatches, and this opportunity of writing to his Commander in Chief was not to be missed. For Richard was well aware that the news he had to tell might have a favourable effect on his future in the navy. Moreover

[1] See Appendix 1

1

the commodore, Charles Knowles, had appointed him to the command of the "Comet", and it was only proper that he should be told quickly of the success of the voyage. So, at last he made a beginning, heading a new page in the ship's leather-bound letter book,

"Comet"

Boston Harbour

November ye 8th 1744.

and with a stylish flourish, began

"Sir."

There he stuck while he thought again. His clerk, momentarily engaged in tallying out stores with the purser, would have to make copies of this, and other similar letters. One would go to Commodore Peter Warren, Commander in Chief of all ships on the coast of North America, and another to Thomas Corbett, Secretary to the Admiralty. There must be yet another to those gentlemen known as the Principal Officers and Committee of his Majesty's Navy. Each would need to be slightly different of course, although they would carry the same news. What a dreary business it was! He had often heard captains say they would rather fight a battle rather than write a report on it, and now he was inclined to agree. Nevertheless it was a duty that had to be done. So he began to write, the dramatic story of the "Comet's" passage to Boston, and her encounter with a French privateer off the Nantucket Shoals.

> "I have the Pleasure to acquaint you that after a very Troublesome Passage and Excessive bad weather, I last Monday arrived at Boston. I parted with Capt. Gayton the 15th October in a very hard Gale of Wind in Latitude 37.00
>
> On the 22nd about seven in the morning being then on the Back of Nantucket Shoals, as I was laying-too refitting our Rigging and mending the Sails which were split the day before, I saw a Sail bearing down upon me under English Colours. I immediately got everything ready to Engage, and kept my men Close.
>
> About eight she brought-too within Musquet shot to Windward of me and still kept her English Colours up. When I found She would come no nearer, I hoisted my Colours and fired two Shot at her, one of which fortunately carried away her Fore stay and

Fore-top Bowline, for notwithstanding his Colours I knew him to be a French Privateer. He then hal'd down his English, hoisted French Colours and gave me a Broadside. We continued Firing at each other upwards of an hour during which time I had the good Fortune to carry away his Fore Tack, Main and Main top Bowline, and shattered his Sails and Rigging very much so that he could not Hale upon a Wind."

His writing was interrupted by a loud thump on the "Comet's" main deck followed by a burst of laughter. Once more he resisted the temptation to go out and see what was going on. The men were in an excited state, and Mr. Bridges was in many respects too easy going, but they had all fought well in the recent action, and a little latitude must be allowed. He waited until the noise died away while he read back through his letter, which had stopped at that splendid moment when he realised that the privateer was so damaged about the fore rigging that she could neither sail close to the wind, nor easily bear away from it. He knew then that with continued good luck they might overcome her. Until that moment his only hope had been to give her a hot enough encounter that she might be driven off.

He allowed his mind to dwell with satisfaction on the tactics that followed. The "Comet's" six pounder guns could do little damage to the hull of the Frenchman except at close range, but from a position astern and to leeward they would have the maximum effect on her masts and rigging. So he had taken up that position, close enough to hit hard but not risking a hand-to-hand encounter.

He wrote on,

"However he made what sail he could from me. I followed him but could not come up with him 'till 5 in the evening when I ran close under his Lee quarter where we kept a continued fire on each other for four hours and a quarter, hardly once out of Pistoll Shot. I could hear the Captain give his orders to board us several times, but I always avoided it, being Night and I but weakly handed."

Richard paused again. He was writing the account in the bald matter of fact style commonly adopted in such reports. But it could not convey anything of the tension of that night's close encounter. The black mass of the French vessel looming ahead of them could be seen easily enough in spite of the darkness, for her hull and sails were patterned against the stars. For brief seconds the flare of gunfire would light up ships and sails and faces, before they were blotted out by the smoke. For hour after hour their senses were assailed by noise, the roar of guns, the rumbling of gun carriages as they were dragged home or flung back, the shouts and screams of men. Nothing he had known before approached it for excitement.

There was the knowledge too that this time success or failure depended on him. If the Frenchman succeeded in laying alongside the "Comet" would be boarded and over run in a matter of minutes. Richard had stood by the helmsman watching every move of the brig. Whenever she tried to close he would keep the sloop away, and sweep her decks with small arms fire. The "Comet's" swivel guns, mounted on the bulwarks had done a great deal of execution among the massed Frenchmen whenever they tried to board.

> "I three or four times ordered all the Marines to fire at her Captain. At last a lucky Shot went through his Speaking Trumpet, then into his Eye, then lodged behind his Ear, after which I found a Sensible Difference in the working of the Privateer. An hour after, she Struck, having her Main and Fore Yard upon the gunnel, her Hull, Sails and Rigging shott all to pieces, one of her Pumps shott away, and six foot of Water in the Hold. About 30 of her Men were kill'd and upwards of 20 more wounded. In Short, I never saw anything so Shatter'd, and I was obliged to lay by two days to repair her before I could make a knot of Sail."

A knock at the door was followed by the entry of his servant who came to light the cabin lamps. Richard waited, glad to rest his eyes while the golden glow spread, reflecting from the polished mahogany of the panelling. Cramped though it was, the "Comet's" day cabin became a pleasant homelike place at such a time.

Alone again, he continued.

> "She is called the "Brador", commanded by

Captain Le Gras, who was bred in the Maltese Service. He is a brisk active Man, and I believe had he not been luckily wounded 'twould have gone very hard with me. She is a new ship, built purposely for a Privateer, but they had cut away her Mizen Mast about 5 week since in a hard Gale of Wind. She is 140 Tunn, had 14 Carriage, 10 Swivel Guns, and had 135 Men when she sailed from Cape Breton; he had taken Five Prizes and had on board 115 Men when I engaged him."

Another pause for consideration. No need to stress the fact that the "Comet" had only half as many guns and men as the privateer. But the bit about the prizes would please their Lordships, for the attacks made on American coastal shipping was a source of constant complaint by the colonists. And this was one privateer less. He had described Le Gras as a brisk and active man, and yet the Frenchman had made a considerable error in attacking one of His Majesty's ships, even one as small as the "Comet". Privateers generally put to sea to find easier targets. However, Richard had been told by the prisoners that when they first saw the "Comet", without a foremast, lying-too in the dim light of dawn, they had taken her for a merchantman, disabled in the recent gales. Small men o' war, and small merchant ships were uncommonly alike even in the best of light. So they had run down on her, expecting an easy conquest, - and so it might have been reflected Richard but for those fortunate early shots that had cut-up her rigging.

He was tired now. There was no need to tell Knowles of the problems they had faced bringing the damaged "Brador" into Boston. The commodore had served in enough actions to know the effect of cannon shot on wooden ships, particularly after hammering for so long at close quarters. Certainly both ships had required prodigous efforts of knotting and splicing, and plugging of shot holes, before they were fit to sail again.

Richard had put Lieutenant Bridges in command of the prize, with a prize crew of the "Comet's" own men. That too had been an anxious time. There was always a danger that when the French had recovered from their defeat they would try to retake their own ship. Then there was the matter of the renegade Irish which they had found among the "Brador's" crew. These had to be brought aboard the "Comet" and chained in the hold. If Richard had his way they would have been hanged for fighting against their King.

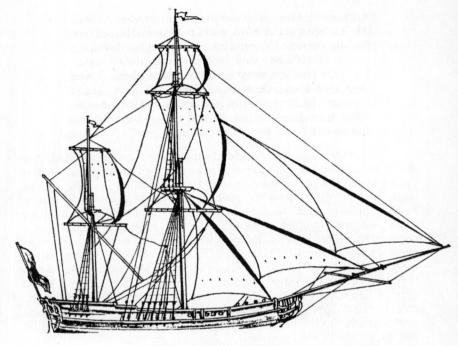

*A Bomb Sloop c. 1750*

In the event the end of the voyage had been quiet enough, and since their arrival in Boston everything had been a matter for celebration. The spectacle of the little bomb-sloop bringing in her prize had caused something of a stir in the port. Boston people depended on the sea for their prosperity and were deeply interested in all seafaring matters. The local merchants were particularly delighted for the privateer had been a constant threat to their shipping. They had already started a fund to present Richard with a piece of silver plate, as a lasting proof of their admiration. There had been a dinner with Sir William Shirley, the Governor of Massachusetts. The Governor who was himself something of a military man had been most complimentary. And of course there had been a regular stream of sight-seers, townsfolk bringing their wives and children to see the prisoners marched ashore.

But the letter had to be finished. He rounded it off with a brief account of the damage suffered by the "Comet". That which had not been remedied already would soon be put right by the shipwrights.

> "I shall be on the Ways tomorrow, and you may assure yourself I shall use my Utmost Dispatch in getting ready as soon as possible. There is another Privateer which sail'd from Cape Breton in company with the "Brador". If I meet with her when I come out, do not doubt but I shall show here the Way to Antigua."

He felt he could be forgiven that last small boast. He ended with the usual courtesies;

> "I am, with great Respect your most Obedient and Humble Servant etc.,"

and that was that. His clerk must make a fair copy tonight, and the other letters could wait until the morrow. He would write home then, to his family in Cornwall as well.

Now he could turn to more practical things. At first light in the morning the ship would be floated upon the ways, and with a purchase at her masthead hove down so that the bottom might be cleaned. That would entail burning off and scraping an accumulation of weeds and barnacles, all of which so quickly flourished in tropical waters. Without a doubt they would find keel and planking and wooden sheathing riddled by marine borers. The seams would need re-caulking and then the whole area thickly covered with tallow. They would be fortunate indeed to be off and afloat again within the week. Meanwhile he must get out and see how the preparations had gone. Besides, he needed fresh air after so much mental exertion. Standing up, his head bent to avoid the low beams, he struggled into his grego, and went on deck.

## CHAPTER II

## THE MAKING OF A SAILOR

The skill and confidence which enabled young Captain Spry, first to beat off, and then subdue, a more experienced captain in a more powerful vessel, were qualities a long time in the making. Although we have a voluminous correspondence to give us a picture of the mature captain, to understand the slow process by which he became that man we have to rely largely on our knowledge of the times and places in which he lived.

There can never have been much doubt in the boy's own mind that one day he would go to sea. Ships and their traffic on salt water had filled his eyes since they first opened, for the tides of a Cornish creek carried them to the very doorstep of the house where he was born. This was at Place House in St. Anthony in Roseland, one of those enchanted corners of Cornwall where water and land are inextricably interwoven. His father's estate stretched on the one side along the shores of the creek and haven of St. Mawes, and on the other above the open waters at the mouth of the English Channel. Between the river on the north side, and the sea on the south, the fields tumbled steeply down the sides of St. Anthony Head, where it overlooked the entrance of Falmouth Harbour.

A would-be mariner could hardly have chosen a better place to be born, and it is easy to see why Richard Spry would show at an early age, a strong interest in ships and the sea. Coasting vessels made good use of the harbour of St. Mawes that lay in front of the house. It was good holding ground, although somewhat shallow for bigger ships, and was sheltered from all but the strong westerlies. When winds did blow hard from that quarter, there was always safety further up Percuil River. A map of the time, drawn for the Spry estate, shows a fleet of small vessels lying off Place, largely the smacks and schooners, brigs and brigantines which made up the coasting trade of the time. Most of them would be awaiting a fair wind, or the tide to take them up the main river to Truro, or to the tin loading berths of Carnon river.

But there was another reason why Richard's interest in ships should grow. He would learn at an early age that one day his brother Arthur would inherit his father's estate, and a younger son would have to look elsewhere for a living. His father's interest in tin and shipping might have been sufficiently prosperous to offer him a future in Plymouth, but would hardly appeal to a spirited youngster, brought up in the freedom of Roseland.

The Sprys had been landowners and farmers in the West Country since the 12th century, and Arthur Spry, Richard's great grandfather had moved from Devon to the manor of Place in 1635. The house was already old, for it had been built in early Tudor times on the site of a small grange which before the Dissolution of the Monastories had been occupied by monks from the great priory of Plympton, St. Mary in Devon. The position was a choice one, overlooking a good landing place, deep in the hollow of hills which sheltered it from every wind that blew. There was little left of the original building however, there being only one room in the house, and the crumbling remains of a medieval church. This was now a private chapel which belonged to Place manor, although it also served as the parish church.

The house itself, of grey and yellow stone, was closely beset with herb and willow gardens, dove cotes, beehives and apple orchards. Immediately before it lay a shallow lagoon, partly cut off from the creek by a causeway on which stood the mill-house of a tidal mill. Into the pool made by the causeway the flood tide was allowed to run, and having filled it, was used to drive the mill wheels as it flowed out. The corn ground at Place sea-mill went not only to feed man and beast in the Roseland, but to provide barley for beer and bread for the ships that lay for weeks on end in the harbour. From time to time small coasting vessels came into the mill-quay with supplies for the house and the village, and took away the produce of the farms.

On a hill top above the house lay the Barton farm. It rested on a south facing fold of ground, and overlooked fields where barley ripened, and sheep and bullocks grazed along the cliff tops. There was barely a field in all that farm which did not touch salt water at some point.

Place and its small neighbouring hamlet of Bohortha formed the centre of a self-sufficient community. It was isolated even by Cornish standards, for it was only joined to the rest of Cornwall by a narrow neck of sandy land, a hump not more than a few hundred yards wide. Across the narrow belt went the only road of the parish. It ran to the north and east, narrow rocky and rutted, straggling between ragged thorny hedges. It joined Bohortha and Place with the village of St. Gerrans four miles away.

In summer this road was passable on horse or foot, and farmers would bring their loads of seaweed or sand on the backs of mules, or drag them along on an ox-drawn sledge. In winter it became a quaggy stream, only usable on foot. Those were the times when a boat was the only good means of getting in or out of St. Anthony parish.

The men of Bohortha were either land workers or fishermen, or often a mixture of the two. Most of them owned a small rowing boat which they kept in the cove fronting Place House. This was the main landing, for just across the creek lay the village of St. Mawes, and barely a league away across Carrick Roads was the fast growing town of Falmouth. From here, too, the creeks went fingering their way inland, to the north and to the west, winding mile upon mile to old river ports, to Penryn and Tregony and Truro. Thus by means of your boat you might get easily to any other part of Cornwall, or indeed the rest of the world.

Into this interwoven land of creeks and hills, George Spry had brought his bride, Mary Bullock of Helston, in 1711. Three years later his first son Arthur was born, and the following year Richard. Thereafter there came three daughters, Lucy, Mary and Charity, nicely spaced at two year intervals. Life for the Spry family must have been on the whole a pleasant, sheltered and yet interesting one. George led a busy existence for he had not only his estate at Place but land in other parts of Cornwall, and his business in Plymouth called him away from time to time, while Mary Spry had enough to occupy her days in the running of a large house and family. For the children there were all the fields and woods and beaches of the parish as their playground.

The young Spry's formal education must almost certainly have followed the pattern for a landowner's family in such an isolated part of the country. They would learn to read and spell, and later write, at their mother's knee, first from a horn book which taught them the Alphabet and the Lord's Prayer, and then from the Catechism and certain parts of the Bible. Later again there could be other improving books, such as the popular "Token for Children" by James Janeway, these being full of stories of the conversion, and the holy living and holy dying of young people.

In time, around the age of seven or eight, their father would be expected to take a larger share in their education, aided by one of the local clergy. Here it could be either the Reverend John Grant or John Wilcocks, then rectors in St. Gerrans. From these they might expect instruction in languages, particularly the Classics, but also English and French. Their father could help with accountancy, some mathematics, and perhaps history and geography. Certainly attendance at the local grammar school in Truro would have been a most difficult and expensive matter to arrange.

There is little to suggest that the Spry children had anything but a happy childhood. The great influence on educational thought in the early 18th century was that of the philosopher John Locke. He recommended that children should have plenty of open air, and exercise and sleep, a plain diet, no wine or strong drink, and, .... "head and feet kept cold and feet often used to cold water and exposed to wet." Certainly that was easy to arrange in a home such as Place, for the children would be in and out of boats and salt water at all times and in all weathers. It was a necessary part of their education, giving them them the ability to take themselves at an early age into St. Mawes or Falmouth.

The boys may have missed the team games, the football and cricket and hurling that others could have, but the woods of Roseland were full of game, and before long they were able to follow the traditional country gentleman's pursuits of shooting and fishing.

By this time Richard's character had taken the form that became so apparent in his letters. He was of a cheerful gregarious nature, anxious to please, and far more interested in practical than intellectual pursuits. No doubt his amiable nature would be fortified by the sort of teaching given by his parents and tutors. This would have pointed out the need for good order and civilised behaviour, as well as a proper respect for authority and men of property. The 18th century was an age of sharp class distinction, between the gentry who had, and the rest who had not. The division was marked in part, of course, by money, but above all by the possession of land. Since the Sprys counted among their relations most of the local landowners, it must have seemed a very reasonable argument, and one the children would quickly learn to accept.

During services in the chapel attached to the manor, the children had around them the family memorials of slate and marble. Many of them bore the Spry coat of arms, a gold chevron and two bars on a blue field. The crest was a dove standing on a knotted serpent, with the motto "Soyez Sage et Semple". There is not doubt that the injunction to be wise and without harm is directly inspired by Christ's words from St. Matthew's Gospel[1]. The influence such a motto would have on a growing boy is difficult to assess. But we know that Richard was fast growing into a determined young man of clear cut principles, and a strong sense of duty.

The Sprys were well aware that their peaceful existence did not extend far beyond the boundaries of their parish. Many other parts of Cornwall, particularly the mining districts of Breage and St. Day had long since earned a reputation for violence. At times of depression in the tin mines, or after a bad harvest, the half-starved miners were prone to go rampaging in gangs looking for bread or grain. Tales were common of armed bands arriving at such ports as Penryn or Truro, or crossing the Fal at King Harry Ferry into the corn growing districts of the Roseland, holding up ships, breaking into stores and granaries, - incidents which generally ended with many broken heads, and some of the leaders hanging.

The most exciting tales, however, would come from Mary's relations at Helston, particularly when it concerned a shipwreck. Every winter a score of fine vessels were driven ashore on the south coast of Cornwall, notably in Mount's Bay to the west of the Lizard. At such times hundreds of tinners assembled on the cliffs and followed the embayed vessel as she tried to beat off shore. They would be armed with axes, crowbars and picks, and the moment the vessel struck they swarmed aboard. They gave little help to the crew but set about cutting, slashing and breaking, so that within a tide a fine ship could become a broken hulk with her masts, sails and cargo distributed around the countryside. Even the power of local magistrates was not enough to stop the wreckers.

Such stories were of particular interest to the Sprys, for George, as lord of the manor at St. Anthony, held rights of wreck on his part of the coast. True, with such a safe haven as Falmouth close at hand there was little profit in it, generally not more than an old barrel or spar or smashed ship's boat. Nevertheless, Arthur and Richard must have nurtured hopes that some south easterly gale would bring a fine merchantman ashore, with all the attendant easy pickings. Equally, there can be little doubt that their father would feel compelled to discourage such fancies. For as squire of St. Anthony he was also local J.P. and as such was bound to disapprove of wrecking, or attacks on property of any kind.

[1] St. Matthew X v.16. "Be ye therfore wise as serpents and harmless as doves."

George Spry emerges as a strict somewhat puritanical figure, fond of his family and careful of his estate. He worked hard to maintain them all, for there were many demands on his income. He had two boys to finance, and one day there would be dowries to find for the three girls. Moreover the manor house now called for constant repairs, as did the fabric of the family chapel. He managed well enough but it was largely due to his interests in Plymouth, and by such extra activities as running the grist mill at Place.

St. Mawes village, no more than a few minutes by boat across the creek from St. Anthony, is today regarded throughout Cornwall as a

*St. Mawes Harbour by J. M. Turner*

millionaire's paradise. Renovated cottages and modern villas spread along the hillsides, sheltered from the wind, and in the eye of the sun. It is a thriving place, its economy depending on the wealth of the retired and the holiday maker. But Richard Spry knew it as a busy borough town which looked to the sea for its living. It was governed by a mayor or portreeve, and a group of burgesses, and since the days of Elizabeth I had sent two members to parliament.

Protected by a small castle, a collection of fish cellars, warehouses and thatched cob cottages was perched above a granite quay, and from there straggled up a narrow valley. There were a few bigger houses which belonged to merchants and landowners, as well as several small inns. Most of the inhabitants were fishermen, and as Richard grew older he would find a welcome among them. Distinctions of class were not so very marked among the Cornish coastal men. He could join them in their small lug-sailed boats, working the various grounds in Falmouth bay, laying crab pots, hand lining for pollock, drifting for herring. In winter time they went dredging for oysters on the shallow banks of the upper reaches of the Fal.

But the time of greatest activity came at the end of summer. This was when the enormous mackerel and pilchard shoals swarmed into the bays and creeks of the south west. They were taken in vast quantities in the seine nets which had been kept ready for use in the fish cellars behind the harbour. For a few frantic weeks the St. Mawes' seiners would be out in West Bay drawing their nets around the silvery hordes, the boats bringing in millions of fish. There followed an equally frantic time ashore, when night after night the pilchards were cured in salt and pressed in barrels. The result of all this work provided food for the poor of Cornwall in the winter, and formed the basis of an export trade to the even poorer peasants of the Mediterranean countries.

The seine fishing called for big boats, some of them forty feet long, and for huge nets which spread over hundreds of square yards, and weighed about three tons. Each seine needed at least three boats, and many hands to operate them, as well as scores of items of gear, - salt, barrels, baskets, buckets, wheelbarrows and so on. It was all beyond the pockets of most fishermen, so it was managed as a company, generally financed by the wealthier men in the community.

Naturally, George Spry owned one such seine. He had his own boats and cellars too, on the beach at Place. Here at the height of the season, the carrying, bulking, salting and pressing of fish went on day and night, with men, women and children employed in it. It is easy to see that Richard would delight in the excitement of those times when he could go out in the boats, learning the craft of the fisherman, and the handling of boats and nets and gear.

There was also a bigger sailing boat owned by the family, a half decked cutter which George would use when business trips took him to Falmouth or Truro. It was often used as a market boat, carrying corn and sheep to the other side of the harbour. The cutter was looked after by an old seafarer, one of those described in the parish registers as "watermen", of which several lived on the Spry estate. Such a one was an ancient who had spent years away in merchant ships and privateers, but was glad enough now to live a quiet life as a boatman and ferryman to Place House, occasionally helping his sons with the fishing.

It is reasonable to assume that Richard joined in the trips to Falmouth. They would beat away to the westward, sailing among the big vessels that anchored in Carrick Roads. The roadstead here had always been famous as a harbour of refuge, and the building of Pendennis and St. Mawes Castle in Tudor times had made it even safer. In the Middle Ages Penryn had been the chief port, and then there had only been the Killigrew manor house of Arwenack close to the harbour entrance, with the two small hamlets of Smithick and Penny-come-quick nearby. But in the comparative peace after the Civil War, Falmouth had developed into a thriving port.

Now, behind the shelter of a sand bar men had built granite quays and a small wet dock. The main streets of the town with shops devoted to the needs of seafaring men stretched along the waterfront, and up the steep hills behind the parish church. Wherever you went there would be the sight and sound of ships; vessels building, or being repaired; with blockmakers, sailmakers, riggers and ropemakers at work.

Most important of all were the packet ships. Some forty years before, Falmouth had been appointed the chief station for His Majesty's mails. By now there was a fleet of smart well-manned vessels carrying mail, passengers and bullion to the Spanish Peninsula and to America and the Mediterranean. The stories of their fast passages and heroic actions against pirates and privateers were already becoming local legends.

There were times when the whole stretch of Falmouth harbour became a sight of fine ships. Into Carrick Roads sailed merchantmen from all the coasts of Europe from the Baltic to the Mediterranean. They filled the space between Pendennis and Trefusis with a clutter of spars and long bowsprits and jib booms. Here came high-sided, richly ornamented Spanish vessels, mingling with low, wide-beamed and shallow craft from the United Provinces. Once, running for shelter from a near hurricane the whole fleet of the Dutch East India Company arrived occupying the anchorage with sturdy ships and sturdy crews, more like men o' war than merchantmen. Richard, sailing among the anchored vessels would soon learn to distinguish the various types, the cats, the pinks, the snows and the barques that formed the mass of cargo carriers of the time.

The harbour was also used as a base for a squadron of frigates of the Channel Fleet and on an occasional port of call for bigger naval vessels. At times Richard must have seen columns of such ships running for the harbour before a fresh S.W. wind. The warships of the 18th century had discarded much of the decoration of earlier days, but had gained a new grace of line. They still presented a pattern of bright colours, black wales of heavier planking contrasting sharply with their yellow topsides, and the chequered rows of red gun ports. Overtopping all were the towers of white canvas, making a brave sight as they sailed in, flags flying, guns firing ceremonial salutes. It would be hardly surprising if such a spectacle decided Richard Spry that he too must go to sea in the Navy.

For some reason which we shall never know, he was late in joining the service. But in 1732 his father died, aged only forty-six, and left the estate to his eldest son. Mary Spry with five children to care for, and only the rents from the property to maintain her household, was probably glad to get Richard's future settled. Within the year, at the age of sixteen, he was entered aboard H.M.S. "Exeter" at Plymouth, under Captain John Yeo, as a volunteer per order.

There were various ways of entering the naval service, but if you had the right connections the most promising was as a Captain's "servant". Alternatively, youths of good family were encouraged to volunteer as royal nominees, and hence were known as "King's letter boys" or volunteers per order. They would be required to serve a sort of apprenticeship, first as a seaman, then as a midshipman or master's mate, and finally after six years at sea they would take an examination for lieutenant. As ever in the 18th century, there were short cuts for those who had "interest", or influence in high places.

H.M.S. "Exeter" was a fourth rate of 60 guns, an ageing vessel, having been built at Portsmouth forty years before. From the moment Richard Spry climbed through the entry port on to her snowy deck he had entered into a life different in every way from the one he had led hitherto. He had exchanged the wide-ranging freedom of his late father's estate for the bulwarks of a wooden ship, 150 feet long and 40 feet wide. His living quarters were on the orlop, the lowest deck of all, where he slung his hammock alongside the midshipman's berth. It was a dark hovel crammed with half a dozen other young gentlemen, aged between twelve and twenty. As a volunteer seaman, soon to become midshipman himself, he received certain privileges, and more considerate treatment than the seamen before the mast. Nevertheless in a man o' war crammed with nearly 350 men, even the junior and warrant officers were hardly better accommodated than the rest of the hands. Richard came under the strict and sometimes harsh discipline that was common to the service. He ate the same food as the seamen, a monotonous diet that largely consisted of salt meat, weevily biscuit and dried vegetables, of a quality that varied from poor to bad.

The training of a volunteer is interestingly set out in a letter which Richard Spry was to receive himself some years later when he was a captain.

"You are to take care he applies himself to the duty of seaman, and he is to have the Privaledge of walking the quarter deck. You are to allott him a propper place to lie in without setting up any Cabin, and you are to rate him Volunteer per order which will entitle him to Able Seaman's pay[1].

You are to oblige him to keep a Journal and to draw the appearance of Headlands, Coasts, Bays, Sands Rocks and suchlike, and you re to take care that the Master, Boatswain and Schoolmaster do instruct him in all parts of learning that may qualify him to do the duty of Able Seaman and Midshipman.

After two years Service at Sea you are to rate him Midshipman if he shall qualify for it. When your ship shall be at Spithead or in Portsmouth Harbour you are to direct him to attend the Mathematical Master in order to further his improvement in the Mathematics[2], and likewise to attend the lessons given by the other teachers, and by the Officers of the Yard

---

[1] 22/6 per month.
[2] The Royal Naval Academy had been founded in Portsmouth in 1729

who are directed to instruct him Gratis.

He is likewise to carry his Journal to the Mathematical Master, in order to his examining the same and representing to us how he has improved himself.

And at the end of his Service in the Ship under your Command you are to give him such a Certificate of his Sobriety Diligence and Skill in the Profession of a Seaman as he shall deserve, as also of the length of time he has served with you either as a Volunteer per order, or Midshipman."

This letter from Admiral Anson was doubtless a counsel of perfection. It was a scheme designed to produce good practical seamen, but not all volunteers received the treatment or instructions set out in the orders[1]. There were captains who concerned themselves with the training and welfare of their young gentlemen, and there were others who regarded them as a necessary nuisance.

The requirement that the volunteers should keep a Journal, and draw coastal features is of interest. It was not intended to encourage their literary or artistic abilities, however, but to improve their skill in navigation and pilotage. The journal was in effect a log book connected with the "day's work" or progress of the ship, and the drawings of headlands and rocks was intended to help fix coastal details in the young sailor's mind.

We have no reason to suppose that Richard Spry had any cause for complaint aboard the "Exeter", although if he had any visions of voyaging to tropical islands he was disappointed. These were times of peace, and it was not the practice to risk the bigger ships at sea during the winter gales. Thus the greatest extent of Richard Spry's first voyage was a short summer cruise to Portsmouth where the "Exeter" lay in Spithead for many weeks. By October she was back on her moorings in the Hamoaze.

Nevertheless the cruise gave the hands exercise in sail handling, and the mooring and unmooring of a big vessel. Much general seamanship could be acquired in harbour but the complicated leads of

---

[1] The Honourable Samuel Barrington, a contemporary of Spry, who had a distinguished career in the Navy as Captain and Admiral, once complained that he had served five years as a volunteer during which he received no pay at all.

the running rigging, the use of halliards and braces, tacks and sheets, buntlines and clewlines, could only be learned in a ship at sea. Moreover it was a welcome change from the usual work of scraping and oiling the masts and yards, polishing brass, tarring the rigging and holystoning decks. In that short voyage Richard learned much about the setting and trimming of square sails, and how to hand, reef and steer. And he used his privilege of "walking the quarterdeck" to study under the Master, the rudiments of coastal navigation, the use of charts, how to take bearings and lay off courses.

The Hamoaze where the "Exeter" lay at her winter moorings is that broad salt water creek near the mouth of the River Tamar. Until the beginning of the 18th century only a scatter of houses had grown along its shores, from Mount Edgcumbe overlooking Plymouth Sound, to the ancient seaport and ferry crossing of Saltash. The centre of local trade was then at Plymouth Town and around the Cattewater, two miles away.

There around Sutton Pool had grown the ancient town, under the lee of the Hoe, and protected by the fortifications of the Citadel and St. Nicholas Island. The crowded harbour was surrounded by cobbled quays, fish cellars, warehouses, and closely packed dwellings. But Sutton Pool was too small for bigger ships, and while Plymouth Sound made an excellent anchorage in westerly weather, it could become a desperate trap in southerly gales.

With the growing need to service a western squadron, the Admiralty had begun to construct a naval dockyard on the eastern shores of the Hamoaze. This became known as "Plymouth Dock", and continued to be so called for long after Richard Spry's time[1]. By the middle of the 18th century, "Dock" was becoming a major part of Plymouth's economy, although for long it was regarded with hatred and derision by many Plymothians. Here was built a dry dock that could take the biggest first-rate, as well as a basin to hold two smaller men o' war. Here also were two building slips for the construction of 60 gun ships, and wharves and storehouses for the loading and repair of others.

The dockyard complex was surrounded by a wall about a mile long, and within it lived the Commissioner of the Dockyard, a senior naval officer of some importance. He was housed in an attractive if cramped corner, laid out in trees and walks, and alongside him lived his underlings, the officers in charge of the many departments. Together

---

[1] It was named Devonport in 1824.

they ruled over the long working days of some four hundred men, labourers, artisans and apprentices; shipwrights, sawyers, blacksmiths, caulkers, riggers and sail-makers. The busy restless enclave was noisy with the hammering of caulkers and smiths, rich with the smells of wood, pitch and resin, and bustled with the movement of men, horses and oxen.

The influence of such an anthill of industry soon spread over its walls. It was surrounded by a rapidly growing town of over three thousand people, all of whom had some connection with the Navy. This was a place of narrow streets and alleys, threading between plaster and slate-hung houses and shops, where lived merchants and seamen, artisans, lodging-house keepers and prostitutes. There were a few churches and many inns, brew-houses, a hospital for sick and wounded seamen, and nearby an old mill turned into a gaol. Just off the port were moored many old ships, hulks that had been stripped of their masts and gear. They were used to house explosives, or prisoners, or crews awaiting ships, and some with sheer legs required for handling masts or other heavy weights.

For Richard Spry, who had seen only the small ports of Cornwall, and who knew shipyards that built one small ship at a time, his first experiences of Plymouth Dock can only have been exhilerating ones. Like most other naval vessels H.M.S. "Exeter" lay at a buoy out in the stream. There was constant boat work, bringing off stores or workmen, taking officers to the dockyard, carrying the sick to hospital. Richard's marked ability in handling small craft soon brought him to the notice of the "Exeter's" first lieutenant. As a would-be junior officer he was put in charge of the ship's cutter on many of its journeys to the dockyard. He thus became familiar with the vast organisation needed to keep His Majesty's men-of-war in being. He saw the great storehouses, said to contain enough equipment for fifty ships of the line. He saw the mast pond with spars in pickle, and beyond that the gun wharf where there were rows of cannon, and small mountains of cannon balls. Here too was a rope-walk, a long covered space where men spun all manner of ropes from the light running rigging that controlled the sails and yards, to cables thick as a man's thigh that could hold a ship at anchor. Alongside the rope walk were enormous cauldrons where the ropes would be proofed against rot by boiling them in tar.

Such constant boat work between ship and shore, under oars or sail, was excellent practice in seamanship but also excellent preparation for a position of responsibility. Handling a cumbersome cutter in a tideway, with the knowledge that a bad mistake might ruin a reputation or drown a dozen men, made for cool and exact decisions. Although the Hamoaze was complete protected from the sea, the river valley drew the north westerly gales that came roaring over the hills of Cornwall. While Richard was aboard H.M.S. "Exeter", one such storm carried away all the ship's boats, and lighters that were lashed alongside. It also drowned twenty people that were crossing by Saltash ferry.

At the end of the year the "Exeter" paid off and Richard went back to St. Anthony to see his family. There can be no doubt that among his stay-at-home brother and sisters he felt himself a seasoned traveller. As a volunteer, had he wished, he could have left the Navy at that point. But he chose to go with the entire ship's company to join H.M.S. "Swallow" which had just completed a refit. It is evident that in spite of its hardships he was well enough satisfied with the life on which he had embarked.More important, he was already deeply imbued with that devotion to the naval service that soon became the hallmark of all good sea officers.

# CHAPTER III

## THE PATH TO COMMAND

H.M.S. "Swallow" in which Richard Spry was to spend the next two years of his seafaring life, was one of the smaller fourth-rates. She was ship rigged, therefore carrying square sails on three masts, but measuring only 130 feet along the gun deck. She mounted an armament of fifty-four guns on two decks. As such she was too small to be regarded as a true "ship of the line", although she would help to form a line of battle with the bigger ships. But generally the fourth rates were used as maids of all work, acting as cruisers, and taking part in convoy duties.

The "Swallow" was a vessel with a distinguished name in the Navy, for she had fought with success against the Spaniards in the early part of the century, during that conflict known as the War of Spanish Succession. Her most notable action occurred in 1722, when under the command of Captain Chaloner Ogle. Then she had captured two powerful pirate vessels off the West Coast of Africa. These were the "Great Ranger" and the "Royal Fortune", part of a fleet under the leadership of Bartholomew Roberts, generally regarded as one of the last and most terrible of the old style buccaneers. The action had been a spirited and hard fought one against desperate men, and it brought a knighthood for Captain Ogle, and a temporary fame to his ship.

Now in 1734 under Captain Graves, Richard found himself part of a highly organised routine leading the same ordered existence as aboard H.M.S. "Exeter". There can be little doubt that he enjoyed much of the life with its ceremonial flying of flags, the piping of the side as captains came and went, and the firing of salutes as ships arrived and departed. Perhaps he saw in this good order and ceremony an expression of those lessons regarding discipline which he had been given in his youth.

However, he must also have soon realised that in spite of the brave show, all was not well with the Navy. A long period of peace since 1713 had bred a sort of rot, which began in high places, and spread downwards into all corners of the service. There was nothing much wrong with the sea-officers, the captains, masters and lieutenants, nor for that matter with the warrant officers and leading hands among the crews. But there was a deal of corruption and time serving among the higher ranks. Many of the senior officers held their appointments due to political patronage. There were admirals holding "rotten boroughs" or Admiralty seats in Parliament, who were more inclined to conduct in-fighting between Whigs and Tories at Westminster, than take charge of fleets at sea. Old men who had seen better days still clung to power. In Richard's early days at sea the First Lord of the Admiralty was Sir Charles Wager who had made a name for himself with the capture of a Spanish treasure fleet nearly thirty years before. But now Sir Charles was seventy years old and no longer capable of running a great Navy.

Even with a firm hand in control, administration of the Navy would have been difficult. The organisation of the fleet was conducted in water-tight compartments, with their different offices in different parts of London. The Board of Admiralty which had the detailed ordering of the ships was in Whitehall. The Navy Office in Seething Lane dealt with the crews and victualling, while the Pay Office was in Old Broad Street. The big dockyards at Chatham, Plymouth and Portsmouth which had the building and fitting out of the ships were all independent of each other, each with its own Board of Commissioners.

Such a lack of system inevitably led to corruption. Accounts were fiddled. Contractors charged high prices for poor materials. Sand found its way into gunpowder, and diseased meat into harness casks. Rotten rope, "old junk" that had been condemned, was worked back into the heart of hawsers and tarred over to look like new. Even when good material was supplied it was not unknown for it be be condemned by an officer and "sold over the wall" later.

There was pilfering in every quarter. It was especially bad in the dockyards from which rope and canvas, iron nails, copper bars and wooden treenails were stolen in great quantities. There was also a long established practice among the workmen of claiming "chips", that is the waste end of the wood. So much timber was taken under this title, that eventually a limit of three feet was fixed on it, whereupon good timber was sawn into three feet lengths, and in Richard Spry's time it was said that in one month, enough timber to build a small sloop was taken out of the Plymouth yard. Most of the new houses at Plymouth Dock were reputedly built with lengths of timber under three feet.

Such wide spread corruption could not be hidden, and although from time to time men were gaoled or dismissed for dishonesty, the practices continued. The knowledge of them bred an attitude of cynicism throughout the service. Not until after the appointment to the Board of Admiralty of George Anson in 1744 were many of the abuses checked. Meanwhile even would-be honest men found themselves trapped by the system. And although Richard Spry must soon have become aware of this dark, dishonest side of the service, we have no evidence that it greatly disturbed him.

Meanwhile his life aboard the "Swallow" continued to be happy enough. She was known as a "West Country" ship, many of her crew coming from the little ports and fishing villages of Devon and Cornwall. Her muster books show that they came from places like Mousehole and Mevagissey, Bodmin and Penzance, and that many were volunteers. Such men would have been easier to work with than those from the big cities of London or Bristol, and easier discipline must have made for a happier atmosphere aboard the ship.

Life was improved for Richard within a year when he was appointed as midshipman, and moved into the mess in the after cockpit. It was still far from luxurious, for the cockpit of a fourth rate was a small dark and noisome den, twelve feet square, and with less than six feet headroom. Here he lived with the other midshipmen, and the master's mates, in a foul atmosphere that was compounded of human sweat and the stinking bilges. There would be other smells too, such as rotten cheese from the purser's store, and the muddy odours that drifted along from the cable tiers.

With as many as a dozen men crammed into the tiny space there was no privacy for anyone. Their possessions were either hung on nails on the bulkheads, or crammed into their sea chests, which also served as seats. Yet his pay was now raised to £2 a month and he received his full allowance of spirits. The food was better too, for each member of the mess paid the caterer, who was one of the master's mates, a pound a month. This was expended on additional victuals, such delicacies as onions and herrings, tea and coffee. Their food was prepared by a mess boy who also kept the berth clean. Richard was now allowed the privilege of a "hammock man", one of the older seamen, who for a weekly allowance of grog would put up his hammock at night, and in the morning lash up and stow it away.

As a junior officer Richard was taking a larger part in the organisation of the ship. At sea he stood a night watch on the quarterdeck with one of the lieutenants, working four hours on and eight hours off, and acting as officer's messenger. During the morning watch he was sent for instruction in navigation and nautical astronomy. At other times he was required to work alongside the men in order to learn the duties of a seaman. But now he was expected to help keep order among them, particularly when the ship was being put about, or the hands were working aloft. In harbour we find him employed in boat duties, attending on those coming alongside the "Swallow", or taking messages to other ships; supervising watering parties, or those engaged in bringing stores aboard.

The main victualling office and store at Plymouth was at Lambhay close under the walls of the citadel, and near the entrance of Sutton harbour. From time to time boats and tenders from the biggers ships were required to make journeys there from the Hamoaze to collect their supplies of beer, beef and biscuit. Much of this work was now a routine, familiar to Richard from his time aboard the "Exeter", but the passage involved the racing tides of the narrows and open waters at the entrance to the Sound. Such winter trips made under sail formed a good school for a young officer.

H.M.S. "Swallow" lay in the Hamoaze until the early Spring of 1734 when she received orders to sail for the Downs where she was to impress seamen for the rest of the fleet. By the end of March she was anchored under the lee of Dungeness where within a few days her boats had taken "43 good seamen from homeward bound India ships".

The eighteenth century Navy was always short of hands, even in times of peace when many of the ships were laid up, "in ordinary". The poor condition and bad pay of His Majesty's service provided little incentive for men to volunteer, unless there was some pressing need such as poverty, debt, or trouble at home. A few experienced seamen, such as James Cook, saw the Navy as a means of advancement. Some young men were attracted by the payment of bounty money, others by the romantic picture of the sailor in the sea songs of the time. Perhaps half of the people of the lower deck came in of their own free will, and these were the men who would make the best of it, and in time provide the leading hands and petty officers.

The other half were more or less pressed men. Some were provided by the local authorities, the sheriffs of counties and the mayors of boroughs, who were required to furnish a quota for the fleet. Naturally the authorities took the opportunity of getting rid of their unwanted paupers, agitators or criminals. Some from London were known as "Lord Mayor's men", and were the sweepings of the city gaols who saw it as a means of escape from long prison sentences, or on occasion even the gallows. But even such methods did not provide enough hands, and the gaps in the ranks had to be filled by means of the press gang.

As a means of manning the forces, impressment had been in operation for hundreds of years, but it reached its peak in the eighteenth century. This was a time when the arrival of the press gang in a coastal town would provoke terror and anger among the inhabitants. The gang would be under orders to pick up seafaring men, but no one could be sure he was safe. Anyone knocked on the head and taken aboard a King's ship would have to produce a good reason to her captain, to show why he should not continue to serve. It was a method of conscription that few approved of, but those who carried it out were under orders to do so, and saw it as the only way to get crews. Daniel Defoe might reasonably ask "Why should a brute, a mere tarr, a drunken sailor, judge by the force of his cudgel who is, or is not, fit for the publick service at sea?" But no one provided an immediate answer, and the barbarous system went on for another hundred years.

It was in such an operation that H.M.S. "Swallow" was now engaged, and Richard Spry took his place in her boats under the command of one of the lieutenants. Inward bound merchant ships were the best source of good seamen. Vessels would be met off the coast, or when about to enter harbour, by a tender or the ship's boats from a man o' war. A certain number of men would be left aboard the merchantman to work her into port, and the rest were forced into the King's service.

It was an exciting and interesting time for young Spry, for the pursuit and boarding of a merchant ship in a seaway, was one that called for good seamanship. It was not made any easier by the threatened crew of the merchantman, who dreaded naval service and did everything possible to avoid capture. They hid in dark corners of their ship, took to their boats and fled for the shore, or on many occasions fought back.

From time to time extreme examples of resistance would be noted in various journals. Thus the sailors of a Liverpool whaler, the "Golden Lion", newly arrived in home waters, fought off H.M.S. "Vengeance" until the man o' war fired a broadside into her and injured many of her crew. On another occasion, in the River Thames, over a hundred pressed men aboard an Admiralty tender, rose up and having overpowered their captors, all escaped ashore.

Richard Spry was now having his first taste of action, and against his own countrymen, but if he felt any sympathy for the poor wretches dragged away when within sight of home, he never expresses it.

No doubt with his clear cut ideas of duty, and the need to obey authority, he would see it as all very necessary for the good of the service.

The "Swallow" remained on her station in the Downs and cruising about the sleeve of the Channel until the end of the summer when she returned to Plymouth. It was April 1735 before she put to sea again, and once more it was to sail to the eastward. But this time she went to join a fleet of 33 ships in Spithead, under the command of Admiral Sir John Norris aboard H.M.S. "Britannia". When they sailed a month later it was westward and then south into the Bay of Biscay, on a four weeks cruise that ended at the mouth of the River Tagus. This was the greatest company of vessels Richard had been in. Sir John took the opportunity of exercising his fleet at manoeuvres and gunnery, and day after day the drums beat to the quarters and sweating crews ran to their guns, while others scrambled about the rigging carrying out sail drill.

The fleet had come to Portugal to provide an exhibition of solidarity with Britain's oldest ally, suddenly under threat, for the long peace with Spain which had lasted since 1713 was now under considerable strain. There was an increasing number of irritating incidents, particularly in the West Indies, where Spain's claim to the right to search foreign vessels was greatly resented by English merchants. Clearly if war should come the position of Portugal was likely to be of considerable strategic importance.

The Portuguese welcomed the fleet with generous hospitality. The King sent presents of food to the ships, - live oxen, sheep, turkeys and ducks, wines, and vast quantities of oranges and lemons. To men used to a monotonous diet of salt junk and dried peas and beans it was a royal gift indeed. Later the ships moved up stream to Lisbon itself where, as was noted in the "Swallow's" log, they were visited by, "The King of Portugal and 6 Princes with all their Nobility in Guilt Barges, the Standards flying." On every ship there boomed out 21 gun salutes, and no doubt the cheers of the well-fed mariners came from full stomachs as well as full hearts.

For Richard arriving on his first foreign shores, the old port of Lisbon must have seemed enchanting. It was to be largely destroyed by earthquake a few years later, but at that time it was still a fine medieval, part-European part-Moorish city. The "Swallow" along with the other naval vessels was moored off the centre of the town, where a great plaza was surrounded with ancient palaces. Here fountains played among gardens lined with strange trees and flowers and shrubs, and winds from the Atlantic rustled among acacias and palms, eucalyptus and juniper.

To eyes accustomed to small grey West Country towns it must have seemed a blaze of colour. Here the narrow streets had tall houses, some with walls painted in pastel shades, delicate pinks and creams, soft blues and tints of gold and honey. Others were fronted with glazed tiles and carved verandahs. There were splendid vistas of red-tiled, pagodo-shaped roofs, backed by steep hills, dotted with the towers of churches and monasteries. For if Portugal was a small country, Lisbon was the centre of a rich trading empire that stretched from South America to India and China.

The quays where the "Swallow" lay were evidence enough of Portugal's wealth. The waterfront was thronged with ships from many parts of the world, and stacked with exotic merchandise. Labourers unloaded into the warehouses spices and coffee, sugar, cocoa, timber, oil and ivory. But here too came the local trade, for the Tagus was the highway for the country boats. They came down river under oars and sails, high-prowed brightly coloured craft, their decks piled with vegetables, fruit and barrels of wine. The quays formed also a market where barefooted peasants and fishermen brought basket loads of sardines, olives and nuts. Others arrived with laden ox-carts or panniered donkeys, and in the bright sunshine it made a scene of noise and gaiety, vastly different from the small jetties, and narrow streets of St. Mawes and Falmouth.

For the officers of His Brittanic Majesty's ships there was much hospitality among the town's wealthier inhabitants. Richard and the other young gentlemen, as non-commissioned officers would often be included in their invitations. It was indeed regarded as a valuable part of their training, for there were times when the naval officer would have to be a diplomat as well as a seaman.

The "Swallow" lay at her moorings in the Tagus for the whole of that year. Not until April 1737 did they sail again, back to Plymouth where the ship paid off. They had been away from home more than two years, and if little of that time had been at sea, Richard arrived back at Place as a seasoned foreign-going sailor.

He had now been in the Navy nearly four years and although in that time he had never faced an enemy, he was already becoming a valuable officer. He was thoroughly familiar with the routine working of a fifty gun ship, and to his ability in seamanship could now be added an equally valuable skill as a navigator. In the cruise down the Bay and back, he had been able to put into practice under the ship's master the lessons he had learned under the schoolmaster. He was an eager student of navigation not only because it was necessary for his advancement in the service, but because the subject appealed to him as a practical application of mathematics.

The fixing of the ship's position was the constant preoccupation of the master and his mates, as well as the officer of the watch. Every change of course was noted, and at every hour a wooden log-ship was heaved over the stern, and the time taken. According to the number of knots on the line that ran out over the taffrail in a given time, so the speed of the ship was measured. Then the imponderables were estimated; these being the set of tidal currents and the amount of leeway made by the ship. All was entered up, and the ship's progress from noon to noon calculated as the "Day's Work". From this, by the use of the traverse table, a reasonably definite position was obtained. In addition, whenever possible, the officers took the height of the midday sun, either with the long established backstaff, or Mr. Hadley's new quadrant. From the altitude of the sun it was a simple matter to work out the ship's latitude.

Thus partly by estimate, partly by calculation, and at times by a sort of inspiration that comes to most navigators, the ship's position would be found by the master, his mates, and the would-be captains. For the young gentlemen were also required to work this out daily at sea, and submit their journals for inspection by the First lieutenant.

This was a time when a great and general interest was being shown in the study of navigation and nautical astronomy. New and more powerful telescopes allowed a closer study of the stars and planets. The work of Edmund Halley (of comet fame) on the magnetic variation of the compass had enabled seamen to make better charts and produce a more reliable compass. Most important of all, John Harrison had just produced his first marine clock. It was given its seagoing tests aboard H.M.S. "Centurion" on a voyage to Lisbon, in the year that Richard returned from there in the "Swallow". Men knew that they were on the way to solving the problem that had exercised navigator's minds for many generations, - how to find an accurate and practical method of calculating longitude.

Such information was long overdue. There were still men in the Navy who could remember how, thirty years before, a squadron under Sir Cloudesley Shovell had been lost on the rocks of Scilly. It was a navigational error that caused the destruction of four ships and over two thousand men. As a Cornishman, Richard Spry would have taken a particular interest in that dreadful event, and we may believe that the story helped to make him into the efficient and careful navigator he became.

Richard's stay at St. Anthony in the spring of 1737 was a short one Ships were being brought into commission as rapidly as manning would permit, and he was soon appointed as midshipman aboard H.M.S. "Canterbury". This was an old vessel of 60 guns, very similar to his first ship, the "Exeter". She was then fitting out at Plymouth under Captain Charles Cotterill, and Richard found himself back in the familiar winter routine on moorings in the Hamoaze.

In May 1738 they sailed south once more, this time in a squadron of ten ships bound for the Mediterranean. They made a short call into Gibraltar to pick up troops, - men, women and children for the garrison at Minorca, - and then they went on to Port Mahon. There was little doubt in most men's minds that war with Spain was imminent. In any such war Minorca with its splendid harbour would hold the chief position in Britain's strategy in the Mediterranean. Here there was all that was necessary for the maintenance of a fleet, a sheltered inlet very easy of access, a dockyard, a hospital, long quays where ships might lie.

The "Canterbury" along with the other vessels of the Mediterranean fleet was under the overall command of Admiral Haddock. She was at sea for the rest of that summer, cruising between the Balearic Islands and the Spanish mainland, returning to Port Mahon for the winter. Early in the following spring they were out again, this time sailing to the westward to take up station between Cadiz and Cartagena. Admiral Haddock had been given few ships but he had large commitments. He had to be ready to forestall possible attacks on Minorca or Gibraltar, and at the same time maintain a wide stretched blockade against Spanish ships sailing to or from the West Indies. "Canterbury" with a squadron of seven others spent the summer beating to and fro between Lisbon and Cadiz, this part of the fleet based on Gibraltar, and under the flag of Sir Chaloner Ogle. Although not formally at war, during that cruise the squadron captured two Spanish vessels bound in from South America with rich cargoes, valued at over £200,000.

The actual declaration of war came in October 1739, but the roots of the conflict went back over twenty-six years, to the Treaty of Utrecht which had ended the War of Spanish Succession. At that peace the Spaniards had lost Minorca and Gibraltar, and had never ceased from planning to get them back. But the more immediate cause for war was over trade. At Utrecht, Britain had gained a monopoly of the slave trade with the Spanish possessions in the Caribbean, as well as permission to send one ship a year to the rich trade fair at Vera Cruz. This single vessel had been used as a cover for a huge contraband trade between English merchants and the Spanish colonists.

The authorities from Old Spain did what they could to check this outright smuggling. They claimed the right to search vessels at sea and provided a fleet of "garda costas" to do so. Unfortunately these Spanish coastguards frequently behaved more like pirates, ill-treating the English crews and confiscating vessels and cargoes. Although there were many such incidents, - in one year alone, fifty two English ships were attacked, - the case that provoked the greatest fury was that of Captain Jenkin's ear in 1731. Captain Jenkin was bound from Jamaica to England in his ship the "Rebecca", when he was boarded by a Spanish privateer. The Spaniards plundered the "Rebecca", and the reputedly cut off one of the captain's ears, telling him that they would do the same to King George his master if they got the chance. The incident did not attract much attention until seven years later, but it was then used by English merchants to attack the government, and to spark off a conflict which began as the "War of Jenkin's Ear", later merging into the War of Austrian Succession.

For the first winter of the struggle, H.M.S. "Canterbury" continued to serve in the blockade off Cadiz. Sometimes she could shelter under the lee of Cape St. Mary on the Portuguese coast, but mainly it was a matter of keeping the sea to the westward with many of her crew having their first experience of the fury of Atlantic gales. Their only hope in time of the worst weather was to run off to the eastward to the uneasy protection of Gibraltar harbour.

Although there was a far larger number of Spanish men o' war lying in Cadiz, than Ogle could spare for the blockade at any one time, they never ventured forth in strength, for the Spanish Navy also had its problems with manning their ships. Of greater danger to the English vessels however were the Spanish gun-boats. These were galleys armed with a 26 pounder gun which in times of quiet weather could row out and launch an attack on a becalmed vessel. The fear of being so caught prevented too close a blockade, and allowed privateers and small squadrons to slip out from time to time. The English ships beating to and fro off the port were kept in a constant state of preparation, their guns loaded and run out, their crews being drummed to quarters several times in a day.

In the summer of 1740 the "Canterbury" was one of Chaloner Ogle's ships that were recalled to England. The Admiralty had fears that the Spaniards were preparing a fleet at El Ferrol in northern Spain to invade Ireland, and there were new uncertainties about what the French intended to do. Moreover there were not enough ships to defend the home trade. As a result Ogle's squadron was brought home to Portsmouth. They arrived at Spithead in July to find a great fleet assembled under the flag of Sir John Norris, Vice-Admiral of England. This consisted of about twenty-three men o' war and a hundred transports, full of soldiers under General Lord Cathcart's command. Rumour was rife about its objectives, some said it was for the West Indies, others for an attack on El Ferrol. But the most significant part of that fleet proved to be a small squadron of eight ships under Commodore George Anson who was aboard H.M.S. "Centurion". This was engaged on a separate mission that would take it away on a voyage of four years to the south seas and around the world.

Most of the ships had been lying in Portsmouth for months waiting for an opportunity to get away, and down Channel. But the wind hung obstinately in the western quarter and prevented them from sailing. An attempt to get clear in mid-July ended in trouble, with the flag ship being run down during the night by one of the other vessels. At last in September, Anson's squadron managed to sail in charge of a convoy, leaving the rest of the fleet behind.

Richard Spry saw them go, having suffered none of their frustrations. He had other matters to concern him, for after serving seven years in the Navy he now presented himself to be examined for Lieutenant. The requirements of that examination were simple enough. It could only be taken after six years' service, two of those at least to have been as midshipman or petty officer. Then, providing he was over the age of twenty, and above all that he could satisfy a board of captains as to his competence, the candidate was given his commission as a lieutenant, - at that time the only executive rank below captain.

Richard Spry passed his examination in July 1740. There is little doubt that he deserved to do so. Admiral Vernon, writing a few years later of the qualities needed in a sea officer said that

> "He should have some natural courage, but it is
> equally just that he should have a good share of sense,
> be perfect master of his business and have some taste
> for honour, which last is usually the result of a happy

education, moderate reading and good company, rarely found in men raised on the mere credit of being seamen."

We may judge that Richard Spry fairly fitted this description, and soon he had the opportunity of putting into practice what he had been learning for so long. He was almost at once appointed as the lieutenant, (she carried only one), of an eight gun sloop called the "Deptford's Prize". His new vessel was a small Spanish-built privateer that had been captured off the Biscay coast that Spring by H.M.S. "Deptford" and having been given her new name, bought into the Navy. Richard was to spend the next three and half years of his sea service in the "Deptford's Prize", engaged on convoy duty in the Western part of the Channel.

Throughout the eighteenth century there had been a prodigious increase in the use of small sailing vessels for carrying goods and passengers along the English coasts. This was particularly true of the West Country where in addition to a long shore line, there were many sheltered inlets and harbours. Here were brought the heavy materials for the new mines of Devon and Cornwall, - coal, timber and building materials. But here also were carried every imaginable cargo; corn and iron ore, cheese and butter, salt and gunpowder, groceries, medicines, people. Even the money to pay the dockyard at Plymouth was sent by sea. On almost any day, a watcher on the shore might see a hundred sail at once, a host of cutters and smacks, brigs and schooners, carrying the vital trade. Not all of it was coastwise, for many of the small vessels crossed the narrow seas to France and Ireland, their exports of tin and fish, wool and corn being matched by imports of salt, timber, canvas and wine.

Such small, unwieldy merchant carriers as served in the coasting trade were easy pickings for the fast sailing Spanish privateers. These came out from the ports of Biscay, from Santander and El Ferrol, to hover about the Western approaches. In the early years of the war three hundred English merchant vessels were captured in this area alone. Although France was at that time neutral, the Spanish privateers used Breton ports for shelter and fitting out, as well as places to which they might send their prizes.

There was a desperate shortage of cruisers able to deal with these privateers. Sloops such as the "Deptford's Prize" were put on convoy protection service, her area of operation being between Portland Bill and Land's End. Her orders were to cruise within those limits, although she might if thought necessary go beyond them in pursuit of an enemy.

After so many years of foreign service, we may believe that Richard Spry found a deal of pleasure in sailing home waters once more. The great bays that lie to the westward of Portland, Rame and Lizard are as fine as anything to be seen in the Mediterranean. Although based on Plymouth the sloop's commission took her into small harbours such as Penzance and Fowey, there to collect a group of merchant vessels and shepherd them to the next assembly point. Sometimes she would call off such places as Polperro or Salcombe, and fire a gun and fly a signal that would bring a lone trader to join them.

Escorting convoys was a task calling for a great deal of diplomacy, for the masters of merchant vessels were notoriously independent in their dealings with naval officers. They would disregard orders and signals, and on occasion slip away from the convoy during the night so that they might reach their next port earlier. Meanwhile service in a small sloop was excellent training in other ways. As the only lieutenant, Richard was responsible for the entire running of the vessel, both in the working of the ship and its navigation. He had to keep the midshipmen and master's mates up to their duty, see that the helmsmen steered properly and that the log was hove every hour. All parts of the ship and its equipment came under his care; the guns and the rigging, the masts and spars, the hull and the crew. Being a small ship he shared night watches with the master. In action he would command the guns and have to see that the men fought with spirit. His days were long and the work was exacting, but it was good preparation for what was to follow. For in October 1743 after more than three years aboard the little sloop, he was sent as first lieutenant to join H.M.S. "Superbe", a sixty gun ship on service in the West Indies.

The "Superbe" was under the command of Captain Charles Knowles, who had recently been appointed to her, and who was also Commander in Chief of Barbados and the Leeward Islands. As such he was entitled to fly the broad pennant of a commodore. Richard was now serving under the eye of a man who was to have considerable influence on his career.

Charles Knowles was an officer who had made a considerable name for himself, both as an efficient captain, and as a hard man to please. It has been said that, "few naval officers of high rank have been the subject of more contention or more contrary estimate than Knowles". Descriptions of him at the time varied widely. To some he was "vain, foolish, grasping, even dishonest;" to others he was, "a man of spirit, ability, integrity". There seems little doubt that he was both brave and competent, but also that he was so quarrelsome that other captains found it difficult to work with him. Knowles had made a close study of harbour defences, and had distinguished himself under Admiral Vernon in a successful attack on the fortification of Porto Bello. Shortly before Richard joined the "Superbe" however there had been a less successful engagement at La Guayra, which was said to have failed due to difficulties between Knowles and his subordinates.

As first lieutenant, Richard needed all his tact and diligence in dealing with his new captain, and he seems to have suceeded well enough. At the end of that year however, there came to the West Indies, as senior officer over Knowles, a man who was to have even more influence over his future. This was Commodore Peter Warren, recently appointed as Commander in Chief of all vessels on the North American coast. France had remained nominally neutral for the past four years of the war, but she was now expected to declare herself. The new commodore had come to take over the West Indian station so that he might do a double service of protecting Britain's commerce and destroying that of France.

Peter Warren was a completely different character from Charles Knowles. He was a Irishman from County Meath who had entered the Navy as an ordinary seaman at the age of twelve, becoming a "King's Letter Boy" a few years later. His progress in the service had been rapid indeed, he was a lieutenant at the age of eighteen and captain at twenty four. He was a brisk, intelligent and capable man, much loved by the men who served with him. He was particularly popular with the American colonists for he had married a girl from New York and owned land in that state. Now, early in 1744, he hoisted his flag in the "Superbe" and took her cruising among the islands, leaving Knowles to fortify the habours of Antigua.

News of the French declaration of war was not received until May, but Warren had already anticipated it, and ordered his squadron to seize any French ships in the area. Within a few months they had captured three Spanish and twenty-one French merchantmen, bringing in prize money valued at quarter of a million pounds. The West Indian trade was of the greatest importance to all European seafaring nations, but France in particular. Their ships carried to the islands slaves and manufactured goods, and brought out sugar, cocoa, rum and timber. By blockading the enemy harbours and convoying their own ships, the

Leeward Islands' squadron was soon well on the way to ruining French trade throughout the Caribbean.

At the end of May, Peter Warren returned to New York, leaving Knowles to resume command of the "Superbe". Warren had been in close contact with Richard Spry for six months, and it seems had already formed a high opinion of his ability. The "Superbe" continued cruising in the Caribbean. In June she was convoying homeward bound merchant vessels clear of the islands to a point where they might be considered safe from attack by enemy privateers; in July she was blockading Martinique, seizing and destroying small coasting vessels. At the end of that cruise she returned to Barbados, where Spry received orders from Charles Knowles to take upon himself the care and command of the bomb-sloop "Comet".

The orders went on to say,

> "Whereas His Majesty's Sloop Comet under your Command cannot be hove down, so as to have her Bottom completely cleaned and graved to guard against the worme.
>
> You are hereby required and directed to fill your water and compleat your provisions with all the Dispatch Possible and the proceed with her to Boston in New England, and there lay her on Shore and have her Bottom well cleaned and Brim'd and paid with white graving stuff and the Tallowed over all, and as I have Ordered Captain Gayton of His Majesty's Store Ship Bien Aime to Piscatagua for Masts and Other Stores, and he will be sailing much about the Time you do; you are therefore to put yourself under his Command and accompany him so farr as your ways shall lay together;---------"

It is difficult to convey the joy that would seize any young naval officer on receiving such an appointment. Richard was still a lieutenant, although as "Master and Commander" of one of His Majesty's small sloops, he would now be addressed as Captain as a courtesy title. The full claim to that rank would have to wait until he was made "post", which would only be granted when he had command of a vessel of over twenty guns. Nevertheless it represented real promotion, and he was undoubtedly delighted by it. He knew well enough that there were some unfortunates who, being without influence, would remain as lieutenants for the rest of their service lives. Moreover it was clearly a mark of approval from his immediate superiors, and given reasonable luck, further promotion would be sure to follow.

The "Bien Aime" and the "Comet" sailed in company from St. Johns, Antigua on the 1st October. Two weeks later they were struck by a storm that was so violent that both vessels were shattered, and lost touch with each other. Spry wrote in his report

> ---"the deck being constantly full of water we must have inevitably have foundered, had not the Gale fortunately ceased."

He was fortunate indeed, for the "Comet" had weathered a late-season hurricane which had created havoc throughout the West Indies. Moreover, although he was not to know it, this was the beginning of a most successful series of events. Had he not suffered damage and been parted from the "Bien Aime", he might never have met with the French privateer "Brador". But meet her he did, and as we saw in chapter I within a few weeks of taking his command, he had fought his first successful action off Nantucket.

Thereafter his good fortune held, for neither the "Comet" nor the "Brador", nor his depleted and greatly stretched crew, could have faced more bad weather. Thus on a grey November day, with pardonable pride, he brought his first command and her prize into Boston harbour.

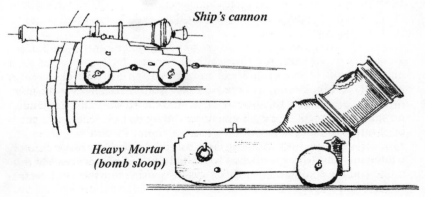

*Ship's cannon*

*Heavy Mortar (bomb sloop)*

# CHAPTER IV

## SHIFTS OF FORTUNE

After the "Comet" had been hauled up on the slip at Boston in November 1744, the work of refitting her went forward at a smart pace. Labourers from the yard were employed in graving and tallowing the bottom, carpenters were replacing the damaged sheathing and repairing the planking in topsides and bulwarks. The ship's company was kept equally busy, scraping and painting, recaulking deck seams, mending sprung spars, and making good the sails and rigging.

Meanwhile, Richard Spry and his officers were dealing with the naval agents and tradesmen of the port, obtaining fresh supplies of victuals and ship's stores and replacing the powder and shot recently expended. Richard had been captain of the "Comet" long enough to know that the command of one of His Majesty's smaller vessels was no sinecure. He had been provided with a list of Admiralty Regulations and Instructions which covered much of what was expected of him. Among his many duties - there were nearly fifty of them, - he was responsible for the inventories of all the stores that came aboard. They included those held by his warrant officers, - the gunner, the boatswain, the surgeon, the purser. He had to see that a tally was kept on the expenditure of provisions, including the daily issue of spirits. He had charge of the "slops", - the store of bedding and clothing that could be sold to the crew.

Above all the captain was required to look after the good order and safety of the ship, and the health of her people. This covered such matters as discipline, cleanliness and ventilation below decks, and in particular the maintaining of precautions against fire. This was the most deadly of all dangers to wooden ships, and the care against it included no smoking (except in the galley), no naked lights below decks, a sentry on guard near the magazines. In truth a captain's task, according to regulations, was never ending and although he had his secretary, lieutenants and warrant officers to see that his orders were carried out, in the end the commanding officer was responsible for the whole vessel and all that happened therein.

Thus the days of fitting out were very busy ones, and Boston was a good place to be so engaged. The greater part of the town was built on a peninsula that jutted out on the southern side of a spacious harbour, where the moorings and the quays were protected by a string of large islands. Within a century the port had grown into the third town of the American colonies, being only less than New York and Philadelphia in wealth and population. Most of the inhabitants were connected with shipping, and the wharves were busy with trade to and from Britain and the West Indies; and even though war was being waged with the French and Spaniards, they traded with certain of their colonies. The Bostonians built fast vessels, and sent several of them to catch fish off Newfoundland, or to go slaving to Africa.

Away from the narrow crooked streets around the waterfront there were many tall red-brick houses, of a style of architecture that reminded Richard of home, with squares and public buildings as fine as those of London. To him the place seemed the most English of all on the American seaboard, for the inhabitants were in general still loyal to the home country, and took from it their cultural standards in their dress and literature and domestic furnishings.

Yet as he moved around among the stores and workshops, the blockmakers, sailmakers, carpenters and coopers, he must have become aware that the men he dealt with were rather more independent and free of speech, than those at home. They all thought highly of themselves. The butcher, the baker and the chandler were as good as a ship's captain, for they had, as Burke remarked, "a fierce spirit of liberty"[1]. Nevertheless, Richard found them kind and hospitable enough and made many friends among them.

The work went well and ten days after being hauled out, the "Comet" was ready for her guns to be brought aboard. Apart from her heavy mortars right forward she mounted eight carriage guns, four each side of the maindeck. These were the usual iron muzzle-loaders which threw, in her case, a six-pound ball for an effective distance of about a mile. The guns were controlled by rope purchases, and directed by handspikes, quoins and wedges. Each gun needed a crew of half a dozen men to load, run out, fire, and clean and load again.

On the coamings aft, mounted on posts went the swivel guns, seven to a side. These were only three feet long and were easily handled by two men. They fired small grape, that is loose shot packed behind a

---

[1] As Richard found to his anger at a later date. See page 119.

wad, or musket balls crammed in a pouch with gun powder. Quickly loaded and easily trained, these were the weapons that had played such a large part in keeping off the "Brador's" boarders.

By the end of the month the "Comet" was lying at anchor again, newly-painted topsides gleaming black and yellow, masts and spars shining, and all her tackle trimly set up. She was ready for sea in all respects save one, that old problem of a shortage of hands. All the usual inducements had been tried, placards plastered around the town with the promises of bounty, and prize money, and a rendezvous set up in the nearest waterside tavern where the master-at-arms might try his powers of persuasion. It had little result, for colonial sailors were not easily taken in, and the crews of British merchant ships kept out of the way.

Early in December, Richard wrote to Governor Shirley, pointing out that he was short of half his crew, although in six days time he was expecting to sail with a convoy to the Windward Islands,.....

> "and as I shall be in no capacity to defend the convoy
> and His Majesty's Sloop under my command without
> a sufficient Number of Hands, I therefore beg your
> Excellency would be pleesed to order your Officers to
> procure me the above mentioned Number of Seamen
> to compleat my Compliment."

Alas for his hopes! Governor Shirley had more important matters to train, and Richard was still there in January 1745 writing to Thomas Corbett, Secretary for the Admiralty that he was ready for sea,...

> "but weakly manned, but I shall Press this night, and
> doubt not but shall compleat my compliment."

Yet it was not until the middle of that month, after six weeks' delay that he was able to sail at last with a small convoy of merchant vessels, and clearing Cape Cod, set his course south for Antigua.

The beginning of the voyage went quietly enough, and on the twelfth of February, three weeks out, they raised the low hills of the island. Here they came up with a naval brig, H.M.S. "Mercury" under Captain Robert Willard. The two vessels had barely exchanged signals when they were aware of the approach of two more sails, coming fast over the horizon.

The "Comet" and "Mercury" beat to quarters, and the convoy made off for the distant islands. Meanwhile the strangers came surging over the sparkling sea, their sails filled by the North East trades. It was soon possible to make out their rig, and estimate their armament. The leader was a ship of about thirty guns, mostly twelve pounders, the other a fourteen gun brigantine.

Any hope that the newcomers might be friendly soon faded. They hoisted Spanish colours and clearly intended to attack. There was little the English vessels could expect to achieve against such superior armament, but they came round on the wind and awaited battle. There was the firm belief among British seamen that any one of them was worth ten Spaniards, and Richard Spry, remembering how they had surprised the "Brador", thought there was a chance that they might be able to do something similar again. If Willard stayed close and they fought a combined action with the bigger vessel, things might yet work out well. Moreover, if they could hold out long enough, the gunfire would be heard in English Harbour, and would bring out some of the squadron to their aid.

The Spanish vessels bore down on them, and after the first sharp encounter concentrated their attack on the "Comet". The "Mercury" although damaged, being a fast vessel shortly broke off the fight and made for Antigua. Clearly her captain considered he should save his vessel if he could, and Spry in his later report of the action said charitably, "I dare say he has his reasons for it, for I take him to be a Good Officer".

Richard now left alone, decided to bear away from the wind intending to delay the inevitable defeat as long as he could. There followed a running fight that lasted for two and a half hours, with the "Comet's" gunners concentrating on the bigger Spaniard's rigging, and again using her swivel guns to keep them from boarding.

But the combined power of forty-four heavy guns against eight was too much. After a prolonged and heavy pounding, the "Comet" was little more than a wreck. All her forerigging, and her topmasts and yards had been shot away. The sails, newly made in Boston, hung in tattered ribbons. Her steering gear was smashed, and she lay like a log in the water. Many of her hands were dead or wounded.

> "In short", wrote Richard, "having not a single sail to set, nor any Conveniency for steering could I set any, I was obliged, though with the Utmost regret to hall down my Colours".

For him it was a devastating moment, but he realised that any other course would have meant the useless slaughter of the remainder of his men.

With the end of the action the Spaniards swarmed aboard. Richard and his crew were hustled over to the bigger vessel, named "La Galga", where they found themselves to be the prisoners of Pedro Garay Cochea, a noted privateer captain from Havana. If Chochea had hoped to make a prize of the "Comet" he was soon forced to change his mind. Naval vessels were observed coming from English Harbour, and he had to act quickly. The bomb sloop was so disabled that he decided to strip her of what he could, and then sink her.

Although Pedro Cochea held a commission as captain of a privateer from the governor of Havana, he was in fact little better than a pirate. The valiant defence of the "Comet" had given him small cause to feel well disposed towards the English prisoners. He had lost several men in the encounter, he had been slightly wounded himself and his ships had been damaged. Now, having taken all that he could move from the sloop, he made off before he was captured himself. Indeed he left in such a hurry that his men failed to scuttle the "Comet" and the vessels from Antigua were able to tow her back to the island.

Meanwhile Cochea sailed for the south coast of Hispaniola where he could find a quiet anchorage to carry out repairs. Little consideration was shown for the English prisoners who were kept short of food and water for several weeks in the dark and stinking hold of "La Galga". Some of her crew took particular delight in tormenting Richard, insulting him and threatening to cut off his ears. It was a black time indeed for him, for he had lost with his ship all his possessions. Among his effects was stolen a sum of £500, this being prize money he had received from his time as a lieutenant aboard the "Superbe". He had managed to hide a little money on his person however, for it was a sea custom not to search an officer when made a prisoner. But all the rest was taken. No consideration at all was shown for the remainder of the crew who were robbed of anything of value. Yet for Richard Spry the greatest of his miseries was the knowledge that he had been forced to surrender his first command, and that ahead of him lay a long period of imprisonment.

Things suddenly improved however when "La Galga" captured a fleet of Dutch merchantmen in the Mona Passage, between Hispaniola and Haiti. These were homeward bound from Curacoa, and they provided the Spaniards with a rich haul. Richard observed, "There were five vessels deeply laden with cocoa, hides and tobacco. One of them carried fifty thousand pieces of eight". The delighted Cochea put prize crews aboard, and set sail at once for his home port.

Havana, strategically placed on the north west coast of Cuba had for long been regarded as the safest and best defended harbour in all the West Indies. It was the port where the great silver fleet, sailing homeward from Mexico to Old Spain, would assemble before making the long voyage across the Atlantic. Here there were sheltered quays, shipbuilding and repair yards, a careenage, spacious stores and warehouses. Within the harbour was a vast inner-basin with deep water, further protected by breakwaters and iron chains and fortified towers. This was where, to the delight of all the inhabitants, who had often suffered at the hands of English ships and seafarers, came Pedro Cochea with his prizes and his prisoners. He anchored in the heart of the town, the ships' sterns tethered to the quays, under the windows of the houses.

The Governor of Havana, Don Gomez Cassitas was also highly pleased with Cochea's success, for as a major shareholder in "La Galga" he profited greatly from it. He decreed that the Dutch prizes should be unloaded, and the cargo and ships sold. He also decided that with the exception of the officers, the English prisoners would be lodged in Havana's gaol along with common criminals. Richard protested furiously about such treatment for his men, pointing out that they were prisoners of war. He had several interviews with Cassitas, who listened courteously, but ignored the protests. Richard and his lieutenant if they gave their parole, would be permitted to live in lodgings and move freely within the town, but the rest of his men must stay in prison.

In spite of his lack of success with the Governor, Richard was soon befriended by many of the Spanish military and naval officers. He was visited by the commandant of the chief fort, Morro Castle, as well as the Admirals Don Antonio Spinola and Don Andrea Reggio. They all expressed their admiration for his vigorous defence of the "Comet", and assured him of their goodwill. This friendship became of particular value later when it was discovered that the Governor planned to send Richard back to Spain as a prisoner. The action was proposed as retaliation because a Spanish colonel, captured by an English vessel from Jamaica, had been sent to England. The Admirals insisted, however, that as Spry was not a member of the Jamaica squadron, he could not be held responsible, and they persuaded the Governor he should be allowed to stay in Havana until negotiations were made for his release.

Richard was also befriended by a number of Irish officers, some of those "wild geese" who had left Ireland and taken service with Spain to fight against England. It was a measure of the ambivalent attitudes of the time, that Irishmen who fought against England at home were rebels who would be hanged for it, while those who served in foreign armies abroad were generally regarded as legitimate foes. Although friendly enough with these officers however, Richard was made particularly angry by one, whose name he gives as St. Mark Forrester, the captain of a Spanish ship of the line. For Forrester had been visiting some of Richard's men and trying to persuade them to serve in his own vessel. Richard wrote later to the Admiralty, with some bitterness

> "I think it my duty to acquaint their Lordships that our English Prisoners are used exceeding ill at the Havana, having very bad quarters, and no more allowed them to subsist on than half a bit a Day, which in that Place is Scarce Enough to Support Nature. After they are brot. very low they are Visited by the Irish Officers belonging to their Navy and Army who take that Opportunity of Decoying great Numbers of them into the Spanish service".

Although he could not get better treatment for his men, Richard did what he could to make things easier for them by spending as much money as he could spare to provide them with extra food. Meanwhile he wandered about the town and waterfront, observing the great fleet of island coasting vessels which brought sugar, drugs and dyestuffs. He noted the well-equipped shipbuilding and repair yards - "they could were they inclinable set four 70 or 80 gun ships on the stocks at a time, but they never build more than two yearly". The town itself was a huddle of red tiled houses, shops and wine cellars, crowded, along narrow streets, with a dozen tall churches; all packed within the defending walls. He observed that the shops, inns and warehouses were richly stocked, catering for the seafarers who had their last fling before starting on the hazardous voyage home. Havana was then famous throughout the Caribbean for its food and drink; - especially for its fruit vegetables and the potent brews of rum.

Richard also took the opportunity to study the defences of the port, for the Spaniards treated him with remarkable laxity. "I have seen most of their forts privately, tho' I was forbid to go near them" he says disingenuously.

It was plain to see that the main strength of the place lay in the great fortress of Morro Castle, armed with 70 big guns, which was built opposite the town, between the harbour and the sea. The port itself was further defended by a number of small batteries and another castle, called the Punta Fort. Yet Richard could also observe that overlooking all these defences was Cabana Hill, a tangle of rocks and bushes, and that whoever held that could dominate the harbour and its defences. Most of his observations were sent to the Admiralty after his release, and with them a copy of a recent and very exact plan of the harbour and fortifications which he had obtained from one of his Irish friends. However he concluded, "in my Oppinion the place is not as strong as has been represented".[1]

Richard's connections with the Spanish naval officers allowed him to collect much valuable information on other matters all of which, in time, he passed on to Whitehall. Thus, he discovered that the Spaniards were very well aware of what happened in the English squadrons.

"Admiral Reggio told me himself the Station of every Particular Ship, with several other pieces of news, which on my denying, he fetch'd a letter and read it to me, giving me an account thereof. I used all the methods I could think of to learn from whom the intelligence was sent, but could get nothing more than that it came almost every week from some Jews who traded from Jamaica......

I had the mortification to see Duplicates of orders sent by their Lordships to Commodore Warren, conserning the Attack on Cape Breton, as Mr. Warren was at Antigua when those orders came to New York. They were sent to him by a Sloop that was taken by Garay Cochea, and not being thrown overboard they fell into his hands. I was shown them by the Admiral who told me he had dispatched a Pacquet Boat to the French at Hispaniola and another to the River Missassipy with Accounts thereof".

[1] This was also the opinion of Sir Charles Knowles who spent some time in Havana later. It is reasonable to suppose that such reports played a useful part in the capture of the port by General Albermarle and Admiral Pocock in 1762.

The Spanish naval officers, and Admiral Reggio in particular, showed a quite surprising lack of discretion in their conversation. They told Richard how all the French and Spanish convoys bound to Havana or the Gulf were using the Windward Passage, and sailing along the south coast of Cuba, thereby avoiding the English cruisers which expected them to use the Old Bahama Channel on the north side. Even more surprising was their disclosure of the manner in which vast sums of money were being sent to Spain.

> "While I was at the Havana, five Sail of their Men of Warr arrived having been at Porto Rico to bring from thence the "Principe", a Ship of 66 guns who was disabled on her Passage to Old Spain with Admiral de Torres Squadron. Who sailed from the Havana last November with 4 men of Warr having on board *Nine Million Pieces of Eight* registered. Admiral Reggio will certainly sail next November with 4 sail more, from 64 to 76 Guns, all new Ships, but sail very heavy. Of the 4 Ships that sail'd with De Torres, only two carry'd any money, the other two were design'd to Stand the Attack should they meet with any of our Cruizers, while those with the Money made off; and Notwithstanding, De Torres went in one of the Money'd Ships, yet was his Flag hoisted on board one of the others to deceive our Ships. Reggio will do the same when he goes home."

It is difficult to understand why the Spaniards were so free with information, unless they thought that Richard was likely to continue as a prisoner in Havana for a long time. So he might have been, but for a curious change of fortune. Early in March two ships had been seized by Spanish privateers off the coast of South Carolina, one loaded with Irish emigrants, the other with Germans, all of whom had intended to settle in Carolina. When the news reached Charleston, the Governor sent to Don Cassitas and demanded their release as non-combatants. This the Don refused, saying as Richard noted,

> "the Germans are not Subjects of Great Britain, neither have we a right to demand them, as to the Irish, he says they are as much Subjects to Spain as to England - therefore he will deliver none of them."

However, Don Cassitas agreed to let Richard and the crew of the "Comet" go back in the brig, which had arrived with a flag of truce to collect the emigrants. That was in early April, but in spite of promises, they were kept back for another two months before finally being allowed to go.

They were away at last and must have been glad to experience the freedom of the sea after the heat, smells and frustrations of Havana. Richard had been engaged in difficulties with the Governor to the very end, largely over the release of his crew. Now there were fresh problems to be solved. He had to care for nearly sixty men who had been half starved for months, and were penniless and in rags. Also, there loomed ominous questions concerning his own future. He was not yet aware that the "Comet" had been saved. He believed that all his service certificates and journals had gone with her. There would certainly be a court-martial on her loss. Although he felt sure himself that he had defended his ship until surrender was the only possible course, yet there was no knowing how others would see it. The ways of courts-martial were notoriously difficult to predict. He might well find himself disgraced, dismissed the service, or at the very least to have ruined his chances of promotion.

The brig brought them to Charleston on the 17th of June. Here Richard set about raising money by drawing bills on the Admiralty to clothe and provide for his men. His own glooming forebodings were lightened a little by the news that the "Comet" had indeed been rescued and repaired and had already been brought back into service. He wrote long letters to Thomas Corbett, the Secretary of the Admiralty, and the Commissioners of the Navy, explaining all that had been happening. To Corbett he enclosed the plan of Havana and an account of the fortifications, and to make sure that they reached him safely, sent a duplicate letter by a second vessel.[1]

Now he set about trying to rejoin Commodore Knowles, for he was still desperately anxious to know his future in the service. But there was no sign of any vessel bound for Antigua. He turned for advice to the senior naval officer, Captain Ward of H.M.S. "Tartar" then lying off Charleston. Ward informed him that a sloop was about to sail north to Boston, and recommended that he and his crew should proceed there to join Commodore Peter Warren who was blockading Louisbourg. It

---

[1] Months later he learned that both vessels had been taken by a French squadron, and all letters had been thrown over the side to prevent their capture. So he had to write it all again.

proved perhaps the best piece of advice that Richard was ever given. When he arrived in Boston he learned that Louisbourg had fallen to the victorious British forces ten days earlier. Another short passage to Cape Breton and he was once more aboard his old ship H.M.S. "Superbe" in Louisbourg harbour making his report to Commodore Warren, and receiving a warm welcome in return.

For Peter Warren, the capture of Louisbourg in 1745 was the greatest moment in his naval career. The port, which was described at the time as "the Gibraltar of the West" stood on a fine natural harbour some four miles long and a mile wide, on the wet, bleak and windy eastern edge of Cape Breton Island. It was a place that was easy to defend in time of war, and easy to enter on what was otherwise a dangerous iron bound coast. The French had founded the town after they lost Acadia in 1710, and they soon made it the strongest fortress on the Atlantic coast. They raised a citadel protected by ditches, ramparts and blockhouses, and inside the defensive walls had built a town of houses and churches, barracks and hospitals, quays and warehouses. Its strategic position at the entrance of the St. Lawrence River, and close to the rich fishing grounds of the Grand Banks soon made it an important trading centre. Ships from Europe, and particularly France, arrived with manufactured goods and wine, and departed with timber and dried fish, and with tobacco and rum that had been brought up from the West Indies. By the middle of the eighteenth century it had grown into a compact town of some 4,000 inhabitants.

In spite of the continual hostility between the English colonists and the French Canadians, many New England merchants traded with Louisbourg. But there were others, notably Governor William Shirley of Massachusetts, who realised the danger posed by the fortress to the American colonies. Shirley was an Englishman who had emigrated to Boston in 1732, a lawyer who by his industry and intelligence had become the leading figure in the colony. He nurtured moreover a taste for military studies, and had long been considering plans for an expedition against Louisbourg. When France entered the war such an expedition had become imperative, for within a few months privateers from Louisbourg had captured twenty-five vessels from Boston alone. One of those privateers was of course, Captain Le Gras of the "Brador".

While Richard Spry had been in Boston at the end of 1744, vainly begging the Governor to raise him some seamen, Shirley was writing to the Duke of Newcastle suggesting that given half a dozen vessels, and

2,000 troops, a successful attack might be made against Louisbourg. Newcastle was in agreement, but as usual time went by and no action was taken. At length Shirley decided to act himself. He persuaded William Pepperell, the richest and most influential merchant in Boston to support him. Then he gained the backing of the Councils of Massachusetts, New Hampshire and Rhode Island, and with it the enthusiastic support of the mass people in those states. He soon had his army of two thousand volunteers, which he placed under the command of Pepperell.

Nevertheless, any expedition against Louisbourg must depend on naval support. Shirley turned now to his old friend Peter Warren for his assistance. Warren, although he received no direct orders to do so, had brought his flotilla northwards from the West Indies, flying his flag aboard H.M.S. "Superbe". In the spring of 1745, while Richard Spry was still languishing in Havana, the expedition was under way.

All went surprisingly well, thanks largely to the tact and common sense of Pepperell, the enthusiasm and courage of his American volunteers, and Peter Warren's able co-operation. On the 30th April the flotilla and its military transports arrived off Cape Breton without interference from the French. The soldiers were landed in Gabarus Bay, a broad inlet to the south of Louisbourg, and advanced quickly towards the fortress. Warren then took his ships to the eastward and set up an effective blockade. He was strengthened by eight men o' war, sent out at last from England.

The French in Louisbourg were well-prepared to resist the siege and expected that help would come, by land from Canada and by sea from France. But the expected help did not arrive. The weather was hot and dry, which was an advantage for the attackers who pressed forward and captured batteries surrounding the citadel. A big French man o' war the "Vigilant" of 64 guns loaded with badly needed supplies, eventually arrived off the port, but was intercepted by a small American privateer, the "Shirley" of twenty guns and a British ship, the "Mermaid" of forty guns. The "Vigilant's" capture was the final blow to the defenders' hopes, and after a siege of only 47 days they surrendered.

The fall of Louisbourg was the greatest success of the war, and the news was received with delight in both New and Old England. William Pepperell was made a baronet and Commodore Warren was promoted to Rear Admiral. Later he was knighted also, and his popularity was demonstrated in many pictures and such typical verses as,

"Urged by her Wrongs, Brittania rear'd her head
And bade bold Warren his furl'd Canvas spread
The Hero rolls his Thunder o'er the Waves
Makes Gallia tremble and his Country saves".

Other benefits came for the victors; particularly for the Navy. It was known that French East Indiamen made a practice of calling at Louisbourg before crossing the Atlantic to the Breton port of L'Orient. Therefore the French flag was kept flying on the citadel throughout the summer, and several deeply laden merchantmen which had not heard of its surrender, sailed into the trap. Prizes worth several hundred thousands of pounds were taken, and Rear Admiral Warren's share was to make him the richest commoner in England.

Richard arrived in the midst of all the excitement of taking over the port and transporting the prisoners to France. But the admiral was not one to forget those who had served with him, and he already knew the story of the battles with the "Brador" and "La Galga". His had been the squadron from Antigua that had salvaged the "Comet" after her action. When the question of a court-martial was raised, Warren stated that as he was a witness of the battle he did not consider this was necessary. For the "Comet" had not been lost and indeed newly restored she had taken part in the bombardment of Louisbourg.

Within a few weeks he was able to show his approval of Richard's conduct in a more tangible way. He appointed him to the command of H.M.S. "Chester", a fourth rate of sixty guns, then lying in the harbour.

This was promotion indeed, for such a command carried the title of "post captain", and Richard was now confirmed in the rank. It meant that provided he could avoid death or disgrace, he would automatically obtain promotion by seniority, and with the passage of time would become an admiral himself. From being an almost destitute ex-prisoner, he had become a person of wealth and privilege. His pay would be raised to ten shillings a day, with the addition of various emoluments and a prospect of three eighths of the value of future prizes. But for Richard Spry perhaps the best of all was the knowledge that the loss of the "Comet" had in no way blighted his career. He could feel satisfied that his superior officers, both here and at the Admiralty, would still hold him in high regard.

Something of this comes through in his letter to Thomas Corbett, in July 1746. Corbett had written to confirm Richard's appointment as Captain of H.M.S. "Chester", and stated that the Admiralty had the greatest satisfaction in his behaviour. In his reply Richard said

> "The Particular Pleasure this instance of their Lordships Goodness gave me I am incapable of Expressing, but hope on all Occasions to Convince them by my Future Actions how desirous I shall always be of Continuing in their Lordships good Oppinion."

That was not just eighteenth century flower effusion, but an expression of heartfelt gratitude.

# CHAPTER V

## H.M.S. "CHESTER" IN NOVA SCOTIA

H.M.S. "Chester" was a fine vessel, built of English oak at Deptford only two years before. The middle of the eighteenth century was not considered a great period of British shipbuilding. The products of the French and Spanish yards were held to be faster and more weatherly, while British vessels, being comparatively unwieldy, were said to be "built by the mile and cut off by the yard".

In spite of that jibe, British warships of the time were lovely to the eye with their bright colours of blue, yellow and red, and their gay gilded carving at bow and stern. They had lost much of the top hamper and extravagant "gingerbread work" that adorned earlier ships, and had not yet developed the enormous bulk of later wooden walls. Nevertheless, there was still a fair display of the wood carver's art around bow and stern; wreaths, cherubs and coat's of arms on the quarters, and a symbolic rampaging red painted lion at the stemhead.

To Richard Spry, his new command looked swan-like among the crowded shipping of Louisbourg harbour, and seemed to be an old dream fulfilled at last. She was not only graceful, she had a grandeur, for she was three times the size of his little bomb-sloop. Her length along the upper gun deck was a hundred and forty feet, her massive beam of forty feet was enhanced by her great "tumble home". Her masts, trunks of fir banded with iron hoops, lowermast, then topmast, then topgallant, soared above the hull for a hundred and fifty feet. Over the bow, the bowsprit and jibboom stretched forward, steeved up some $36^0$ above the horizon, carrying triangular jibs and square spritsail making her seem even half a long again.

From the moment Richard boarded her to the ceremonial twittering of bosuns' pipes, and the salutes of officers and marines, his life had taken a new and richer dimension. His way to his quarters lay along the quarter deck, past rows of big black nine-pounder guns, past the cabins of his lieutenants, to the "coach" under the poop where guarded always by a marine sentry he could live a life of solitary ease.

**_H.M.S. Chester, a Fourth Rate of 1750_**

Now, for the first time since he joined the Navy, he was able to enjoy the luxury of good accommodation. He had a large day cabin stretching across the width of the stern. It was not ostentatious but well furnished with a dining table, writing desk, comfortable chairs, a rounded settee under the glazed windows. Now, if he wished, he could step out onto his private stern walk. Now he could afford to eat well with fresh food bought from the shore, and with his own stock of animals, pigs and hens, sheep or goats kept in the manger forward, well away from his own quarters. He had a retinue of personal servants, cook, steward, secretary, for he was allowed a dozen followers. He had become a demi-god, with all the privileges and only a few of the penalties that go with such a position.

Richard's immediate concern, however, was with the efficient running of the ship. It was a much greater problem than he had known aboard the "Comet". There were under him some three hundred and fifty men, and although he had to assist him a large array of commissioned lieutenants, and warrant officers and their mates, yet he knew well enough that success or failure of the ship lay in his charge.

The Admiralty had always recognised this, for the captain of a man o' war, was given powers of life and death over his ship's company. Although he might not hang a man without a court martial, yet he could have him flogged to such a degree that he might never recover. There were notorious captains who abused those powers, treating their men with an arbitrary savagery that drove them in the end to mutiny. Richard Spry was not one of these. He was one of the greater number of captains who were chiefly concerned to run a 'taut ship', and used naval discipline to that end. But within the harsh conditions of seafaring life, Richard clearly had the welfare of his ship's company at heart. We have already seen something of this in his care for the prisoners at Havana. Now his early letters aboard the "Chester" show the same spirit. He writes to his admiral concerning the lack of medical necessaries for the sick aboard the vessel, none having been supplied for several months. Another letter to the Commissioners of the Navy requests a supply of Slops and hammocks and bedding for the use of the seamen as othewise they were forced to buy them ashore at exorbitant prices "and the Weather is so Excessive Severe that 'tis Impossible for the Seamen to subsist without them".

The weather in the region of Louisbourg was notoriously uncertain, having more than its share of rain and mists. And now after an unusually fine summer there followed a wet autumn and a vile winter. Strong winds and rain were suceeded by fog and snow. At the first onset of bad weather, Richard joined with the other captains in a request to Rear Admiral Warren.

> "As the Weather begins to set in Pretty Severe", (he wrote) "and there's a Necessity for our People being expos'd to work in the Cold in unloading Vessells and other Services for the Garrison we therefore think it would be of Service towards Preserving the health of our Seamen if you would please to order them to be

served a half Quartern of Rum over and above their
Proper Allowance till the Severity of Winter is over".

Like the good admiral that he was, Warren replied promptly,
permitting the men a full quartern of rum or brandy extra, above their
daily ration. This gave them a daily tot of $\frac{3}{4}$ of a pint of pure spirit in all.
It may not have made them much warmer or drier, but undoubtedly it
helped to blunt their sensitivity to the weather and other harsh factors of
life.

Richard Spry and his ship were soon involved in the complex
business of running the occupied port. Rear Admiral Warren, who was
now also Governor of Louisbourg, lived ashore, but hoisted his flag
aboard the "Chester", and orders came to Richard in rapid succession.
The "Chester" was required to supply food and naval stores to other
ships in need, and she was to provide guard boats for quarantine duties
for fear of the introduction of smallpox then known to be raging among
the North American colonies. She was required to receive and victual
French and Canadian prisoners who were brought in by raiding parties.
Among these Richard notes

"there were French Indians who were taken Prisoners
in the Gulf of Cancoa, and by whose means we are in
hope of bringing about an Accommodation with their
Tribes".

It proved to be an unfulfilled hope for these Indians were members of
the Micmac tribes whose territory stretched into Acadia and who
generally fought in support of the French. They were known to hate the
English, and it is difficult to believe that the food and conditions they
met with aboard the "Chester" would do much to alter their
dispositions.

That winter of 1745/46 was to prove particularly severe. From
time to time the sea outside Louisbourg froze, and the ships were
icebound in harbour. With ventilators hatches, gunports and scuttles
closed against the weather, the air below decks reeked with the stench of
close-packed humanity. On the dim gun deck where the men worked,
ate and slept, there was no warmth other than that provided by the
huddled mass of their messmates. There was no means of drying wet
clothing and the lower decks soon became a breeding ground for vermin
and disease. Even the officers who lived in their comparatively spacious
quarters aft were exposed to a deal of ill health.

But if conditions were bad afloat they were even worse ashore. The bombardment had shattered most of the houses in the town. The French inhabitants had been sent back to Europe, but the American troops who remained suffered great hardships. There was a shortage of fresh food and the water in the wells was contaminated. The icy blast drove the snow into their living quarters; sickness followed, and as many as a dozen men died each day. At the height of the plague half the garrison was ill. Resentment led to frequent fights between soldiers and sailors, and at one time there was a state of near mutiny among the American levies who had expected to be sent home. There can be little doubt that if the French had been able to mount an attack from Canada during that winter they could have retaken Louisbourg with ease.

Spies brought news that a large force of 6,000 men was being prepared in Quebec with the intention of such an attack, and preparations were hurried forward to resist it. The walls of the fortress were repaired, extra guns were ferried ashore from the ships, the "Chester's" crew was engaged in constructing a boom ready to haul across the harbour mouth. But although the French Canadians were experts at moving troops across snowy terrain, no attack was made. It seems that the weather was too bad even for them to move.

With the Spring, Vice-Admiral Isaac Townsend arrived from England with reinforcements, and with his orders to take over the charge of the sea forces at Louisbourg. Charles Knowles came up from the West Indies to relieve Peter Warren, as Governor of Louisbourg. Warren was a sick man, and had been hoping to return to New York. But Governor Shirley was already busy planning another expedition, this time against Quebec with his victorious if now depleted forces, and he wanted Warren to lead it. He had received a fresh promise of more British ships and troops from the Duke of Newcastle. They waited, yet as so often happened, Newcastle's promises were greater than the fulfilment, and no further reinforcements arrived.

With the summer life had improved in Louisbourg, and Warren decided to return to New England. Richard had orders to take the admiral, and Sir William Pepperell, with several of the American troops back to Boston. With this load of notables on board Richard weighed anchor on the 6th of June, but even as they cleared the harbour mouth they met the sloop "Hinchinbrook" coming in with important despatches for the admiral. Whereupon the "Chester" was required to put back into Louisbourg forthwith.

The letters from England conveyed the information that it had been decided that an attack would after all be made on Quebec that summer, and that more ships and troops would soon be there. The plan was to send the Navy with extra troops up the St. Lawrence River to attack Quebec, while an army of colonial troops would march up the valley of the Hudson, and invade Canada by way of Montreal.

While preparations for this expedition were being put under way again, Warren sailed for Boston aboard the "Chester". There Richard was delighted to received fresh orders. He was to proceed on a short cruise off the coast of Carolina against any French or Spanish privateers. He sailed forth praying that he might again meet with Pedro Garay Cochea and "La Galga". Although he had no such fortune, he met with, and nearly captured, a Spanish brig that he recognized as one of Cochea's vessels. He was in close pursuit and only the loss of his fore-topmast, due to the "Pitch of the sea", prevented her capture, and finally Richard had to return to Boston disappointed.

He was given instructions at once that would involve him in the war being fought in a small but strategically important corner of North America. This was in Nova Scotia, the peninsula that was separated from the rest of the colonies by the turbulent waters of the Bay of Fundy, and joined to French Canada by a narrow neck of land in the north. It had previously been part of Acadia, settled by the French in the sixteenth century, and after changing hands several times had been lost to the British in 1710.

It was a hard and rocky land, clothed in thick forests. The British had done little to settle it, and in spite of forty years' occupation, the greater part of its population of small farmers and fishermen remained fervently French at heart. They had been forced to take an oath of allegiance to the British crown, but the French connection had been maintained through Cape Breton Island. Jesuit priests from Louisbourg had continued to move freely among them, keeping alive their old religion and their old nationalism.

The people of New England were well aware of the value of Nova Scotia, particularly because of its rich fishing grounds and its strategic position close to their Atlantic trade routes. But the British government seemed to be indifferent. They had maintained only one settlement of importance, at Annapolis Royal on the south-west corner of the peninsula. Here a small fort, originally built by the French and then called Port Royal, guarded the basin of Annapolis. This was at the point where a river of the same name broke through the mountain range that ran north and south of the peninsula, and then flowed into the Bay of

Fundy. It was the best harbour in that exposed and inhospitable corner, where gales were frequent and furious, and the rise and fall of tides the biggest in the world.

Through the narrow entrance into the basin the sea swept like a mill stream, but, once inside, there was a fine shelter in a landlocked harbour. Here the biggest ships of the line might proceed for several miles as far as the fort, and small ones could take the tide for many miles beyond. There were extensive shallows and sandbanks but the deep water channel led to Goat Island, below the fort, where there was a fine anchorage. Here also there was a good landing, and a village of some eighty rough log houses chiefly occupied by Acadian farmers and fishermen.

Although Annapolis Royal was the only strong point in that part of Nova Scotia its defences had been greatly neglected. Cows had been allowed to wander over the earthworks, and had broken them down in places. There was a garrison of only one hundred and fifty soldiers under the control of the Governor, Mr. Mascarene. But if the British government had failed to recognise the importance of the place the French thought otherwise. They had made an attempt to recapture it soon after war was declared in 1743. Then an army of six hundred French Canadians and Indians had moved from the north, and surrounded the place. Governor Mascarene, himself of French Huguenot descent but devoted to England, had resisted valiantly. He restored the defences and though there was some skirmishing, the invaders without heavy guns would not risk direct attack, and settled down to a siege. They had expected naval help from Louisbourg (still in their hands at that time) but none came. Instead there arrived a relieving force of colonial troops from Boston, and the French were forced to retire to their northern borders.

Now, three years later they were about to try again. This time however Annapolis was in much greater danger, for the strategic scene had changed. Since the French had lost Cape Breton Island the year before, they were now more than ever determined to retake Nova Scotia. This done, they might hope to use it as a base to recapture Louisbourg. But first they must take Annapolis Royal, which would not only enable them to control the Bay of Fundy, but would encourage the native Acadians and Micmac Indians to join in the struggle.

Governor Mascarene had news of a large land force of French Canadians and their Indian allies assembling at Minas in the north of the peninsula, and which was expected to advance by land. He sent urgent messages to William Shirley in Boston, begging him for fresh reinforcements and artillery. Meanwhile reports had been received of a French fleet of eight ships of the line, ten frigates, and twelve transports loaded with troops and artillery about to sail from Brest for Nova Scotia.

Governor Shirley's projected expedition against Quebec had fizzled out for lack of support from Britain. That country had fresh fears of yet another invasion from France following the defeat of Charles Edward Stuart, for although the earlier attempt had failed, it had caused a singular fright. Nothing could be spared for Mascarene from Louisbourg which they thought might also be the object of attack. So H.M.S "Chester" newly returned to Boston was hurried away by Rear Admiral Warren to give what aid he could to Annapolis Royal. Warren was in no doubt of its importance. His orders to Spry said that "the Reduction of it would be of fatal consequence to Louisbourg and to all His Majesties American Dominions".

The "Chester" sailed without delay on what should have been a short passage, but in fact became a long one of twelve days, beating through gales and thick fog off the souther corner of Nova Scotia. Richard arrived at Annapolis to find that he was indeed greatly needed. His former acquaintance, the American Captain John Rous, was lying in the Basin, his ship dismasted and badly damaged in the recent gales. Richard had first met Rous at Louisbourg where he had distinguished himself in a small gun brig, by leading the French man o' war "Vigilant" into a trap that resulted in its capture. He had been rewarded for his valour on that occasion with the command of the frigate H.M.S. "Shirley", and it was this vessel that had been in trouble. She had been driven ashore while trying to make Annapolis, and although Rous had managed to get her off and into harbour, he was in great need of repair.

Richard set about with his usual enthusiasm, sending his carpenters and seamen to help aboard the "Shirley", cutting masts and spars out of the forests, and then stepping and rigging them. He supplied rope, tallow, canvas, gunpowder, and within a couple of weeks they had the frigate into a fighting unit again, ready to serve in the defence of the harbour.

Meanwhile bad news was coming from Admiral Townsend in Louisbourg and Peter Warren in Boston. All reports confirmed that a hard campaign was in prospect. The army of Canadians was moving down from the north, and the expected fleet from Brest had been sighted off Nova Scotia. Warren wrote to Richard at the end of September,

> "Where their blow will fall is uncertain but 'tis
> probable from their going into Chibucto[1] that they
> intend to land troops, cannon and Stores there to joyn
> the Nova Scotians and make an attempt that way on
> Annapolis, for the season is so far advanced that I am
> in hopes that they won't venture their ships into the
> Bay of Fundy or the Basin of Annapolis".

He then concluded more optimistically "I hope to have a share in the
Destruction of those Gasconading French Chaps".

There could hardly be a clearer demonstration of the value of sea
power than the manner in which communications were kept open
between Boston, Louisbourg, and Annapolis. In spite of the fact that
the latter place was cut off by superior French forces on land, small
vessels were able to travel in and out of the harbour, bringing
despatches, supplies, and occasional reinforcements. Early in October
Governor Shirley was able to send a force of two hundred and fifty New
England troops, which gave fresh heart to the garrison at Annapolis.

Richards letters continued to show a fine confidence. He wrote
to Warren,

> "If this should be the French fleet, and they attack the
> Place, I doubt not Sir but every Officer and Seaman of
> this Ship will consider they belong to you, and act like
> Men who claim that Glorious Title, for my own Part I
> hope I shall never give you any reason to repent your
> conferring on me the many favours I have received
> already; which I shall every acknowledge with the
> utmost gratitude and make it my Constant Studdy to
> merit your further Esteem".

High-flown sentiments indeed, but in accordance with the
expression of those times, and certainly in accordance with his feelings
for Warren. The esteem was not one-sided. Warren concluded one of his
letters;

> "Dear Spry, I've only time now to tell you I'm
> persuaded if Occasion should offer, you will do your
> Country, Your King, Yourself and me Honour, be the

---

[1] The bay in Nova Scotia, later to be the site of Halifax.

Consequences Whatever Shall Please God. I am with truth,
     Your most Faithfull Friend and Humble Servant
               P. Warren".

     Meanwhile Richard was turning his energies to practical measures against the looming threat. He collected together all the small craft from round about the harbour, and brought them under the fort, to prevent them being used against the "Chester" as fire ships. He pressed the local Acadian inhabitants from the small village outside the defences and set them to cutting the pines along the thickly wooded shore. This permitted the "Chester's" guns to command the only road from the north along one side of the basin. When a small sloop called the "Montague" arrived with artillery stores from Boston he took her under his orders (much to her master's annoyance) and used her for scouting off the harbour entrance.

     There were more occasional skirmishes with French guerillas and Indians. A schooner bringing up wood for the garrison was captured by a band of French Canadians who ran her ashore. Richard immediately despatched the "Montague" to recapture her, which she did without loss of a man. But unable to get the schooner off the shore they were forced to burn her. It now became Spry's policy to take or destroy any boat he could find, for he knew that the only way the enemy would be able to move guns or heavy stores was by way of the water.

     Finally he took the "Chester" to lie off Goat Island where the channel was so narrow that any vessel approaching Annapolis from seaward would find its way blocked. All he could do thereafter, was to continue the regular routine of exercising the ship's guns, taking in wood and water, and wait.

     At this point the Acadian settlers vanished overnight. It was most disturbing, for hitherto they had been very cooperative, cheerfully supplying labour, fresh food and information. The reason soon became clear, when a large band of French Canadians and Indians appeared on a hill top, a couple of miles from the fort. These threw up earthen ramparts, set up their tents, and hoisted a white banner with the golden fleur de lys of France. They were out of effective range, but, as Richard wrote, "both the Fort and I gave them a shot by way of Defiance".

     No doubt it made the defenders feel better, but nevertheless things were looking grim. Annapolis was now completely surrounded on land, and communication between Spry and Mascarene was only

possible by water, their boats having to run a gauntlet of musket fire
from the shore. Richard's opinion was that it would not be possible for
the fort to hold out for long against determined attack. Equally clearly if
a large French fleet did arrive in the basin, Richard's force of one fourth
rate, a frigate and a sloop, while they were well-placed to make effective
resistance, against superior forces, the battle could only result in their
final destruction.

His letters to his superiors show a curious mixture of confidence,
determination and apprehension. To Peter Warren he expresses a hope
of seeing him soon, and joining with him in the destruction of the
French fleet. One of his letters tells us of a vivid dream in which the
"Chester" had captured a large French man o' war, and then goes on in
less fanciful vein to give technical details of how a careening and fitting-
out wharf could be built at Annapolis.

At the beginning of October he wrote to Vice-Admiral
Townsend;

> "You see Sir the Circumstances we are in and will be
> the best judge how to act at this Critical Juncture, in
> the mean time you may be sure yourself I shall do
> everything in my Pow'r for the Preservation of this
> Place, which I am Convinced if of the utmost
> Consequence to all America."

By the same packet he sent an account of his doings to
Commodore Knowles, concluding, "At what will be my Fate, if I leave
this World with the Character of doing well as an Officer and Seaman,
'tis all I aim at."

It is not difficult to imagine Richard Spry seated at his desk in the
"Chester's" great cabin, listening to the run of the swift tide past the
rudder and contemplating the problems of the forthcoming battle.
There was no means of telling whence the blow would fall, whether by
the arrival of some great ships, or by a land force from Chebucto. The
Canadian troops made sporadic raids, but were clearly awaiting the
arrival of reinforcements.

Then on the third of October the whole scene changed. An
English raiding party set out in two small boats, with troops and Indians
from the Massachusetts volunteers, to seek for information. They
suceeded in capturing two of the missing Acadians, and brought them
back aboard the "Chester". Next day Richard wrote a hasty despatch to

Warren containing the intelligence they had managed to gain from their prisoners.

"The French fleet in their Passage to America met with an excessive hard gale of wind on the second of September off the Isle of Sables which separated them and had almost drove them on shore on the said Island, that they were certain two of their Large Ships were lost, the admiral having brot. in with him part of the Company belonging to one of them, and that the rest had Perish'd; that the Adml. arrived at Chebucto with four sail only, and that he dyed soon after as imagined through grief for the loss of his Fleet ..... that sometime after, thirty one sail more arrived, ..... that he spoke with a Canadian lately who informed him that he saw three sixty-four gun ships sail from Chebucto to block up this Place thirteen days ago, and that four days after Eight Ships more sail'd, two of which were Loaden with Mortars, Shells, Cannon and other War like Stores all which are to be landed (if they know how) in order to attack this Garrison; that there were only a thousand Canadians come and that no more were expected, that they have waited a long time at Manis in Expectation of the Fleet from France, and that an officer with 500 men had return'd on hearing Canada was to be attacked by the English, that they[1] had brot. no other arms with them than Musquets; that a great number of Vessells than ever was known and four Very Large Ships was arrived and that Six Sail of Man of Warr were saild from Chebucto to block up Louisbg; a very Pretty Joke indeed! This is all the Intelligence I can pick out of my Prisoner who I believe is very honest and tells everything he knows. Good God sir, if you had but ten sail of ships now how easy wd. it be to Compleat the Distruction of this grand Armament, as all the rest of their schemes have proved abortive I am determined if possible to disapoint 'em in this ..... as 'tis now fine Weather we shall be in daily Expectation of seeing those

---

[1] i.e. the Canadians.

troublesome follows arrive, and you may depend we
are not Idle in Preparing for their reception."

Spry's account, written in his usual tumbling style, was sent also
to Townsend and Knowles, and the "Chester" and the garrison settled
down once more to their waiting and watching, with only occasional
skirmishes against the surrounding forces. Soon after the wind set in to
blow very hard and cold from the north, a circumstance which made
Richard express the hope that "it will make the French shake a Cloath
in the Wind, and think of Putting on their muffs".

He could begin to take a more light hearted view of their
circumstance, for it was now mid October, and he concluded that soon
the enemy would find the winter weather would render an attack
impossible.

What he did not know, however, was that the whole French
expedition against Nova Scotia and Cape Breton had already ended in
disaster. It is a story that for its trail of misfortunes matches that of the
great Spanish Armada against Elizabeth's England. The fleet of French
men-of-war and transports which had set forth from Brest in late June,
under the Duc d'Anville, had run into gales in the Bay of Biscay, and
long calms off the Azores. The voyage that might have been expected to
take around fifty days, took two and a half months. As they loitered to
the westward, inevitably sickness began among the three thousand
troops, closely packed into the transports. They arrived off the coasts of
Nova Scotia in early September, and sailed into thick fogs. A storm
scattered the fleet, followed by more fog. The stricken ships, now
uncertain of their position, crept along the land, beating bells, firing
guns and burying scores of dead.

The Duc d'Anville, in the flagship, arrived at last in the harbour
of Chebucto, expecting to find most of his fleet already there. He was
devastated to find only a couple of transports. A squadron of ships
which he had been told would join him from the West Indies had arrived
before, and discovering the place empty, had sailed on to France.
Although most of his fleet came straggling in over the following days
with their sick and starving crew, the experience had been too much for
the admiral. He died, probably of heart failure, although some believed
he had been poisoned.

The command now fell upon Vice-Admiral D'Estourmel, who
clearly felt unequal to the task, for after a violent quarrel with some of
his officers, he committed suicide with his own sword. The third in

command, Admiral de la Jonquiere, took over and set about trying to restore the situation. Men were still dying every day - English prisoners reported that among the troops and seamen, 2,400 had died at sea, and 1,135 at Chebucto, all of the plague. Clearly, la Jonquiere with his diminished forces could not hope to take Louisbourg where there was still a large English fleet, so he determined to launch at attack on the easier target of Annapolis. He landed stores and muskets at Chebucto for the use of the Acadians and on the fourth of October, the day on which Spry was penning that long despatch to Peter Warren the French sailed once more with 43 ships to the attack. But this fleet met its final misfortune off Cape Sable to the south of the island. Here a fierce northerly gale scattered them once more. Some returned to Chebucto, some made for the West Indies, only two arrived off Annapolis, and there realising the hopelessness of trying to enter the harbour in face of the "Chester" and "Shirley", retired to Chebucto also. Here De la Jonquiere gathered together his remaining ships and sailed for home. Only at the end did his luck change. His fleet met a Dutch merchantman who informed them that a powerful force under Anson was blockading Brest, and they managed to evade this and escape into Rochefort.

For Spry and Mascarene the first signs that the danger had passed came on the twenty-third of October, when the Canadian troops suddenly left their camp and began to march back up the road to Minas. The Acadian peasants re-appeared in their village, and life aboard the "Chester" returned once more to its normal round.

Soon there came orders from Rear Admiral Warren for the "Chester" to join him at Boston, and Richard's part in the Annapolis campaign was over. There had been no real fighting, and the French had been mainly beaten by those old allies of England, the wind and the sea. But there can be little doubt about the reality of the threat to the defenders of Annapolis.

Charles Knowles observed later, "Could the French have arrived timely, and brought their people in good health, I think they would have succeeded without any great resistance." Therein he did Spry, Mascarene and their mixed band of British seamen and New England volunteers an injustice, for as we have seen, they were determined to resist whatever forces came. Nevertheless, we can be sure that Annapolis would have fallen before such a massive assault, and that would have been a signal for the Acadians to rise all over Nova Scotia. Such an event might well have altered the course of American history.

Richard was conscious of the importance of the part H.M.S. "Chester" had played, and he was well satisfied with the result. He returned to Boston to receive tributes from his senior officers. Shortly he was given orders for home, and after a slow passage arrived in Spithead at the end of December, where the ship was put into dock to be cleaned and refitted. Richard was told he could give ten days' leave to such men as he could trust, or to those who had large sums of pay owing to them. The rest were to be distrubuted among the other ships in the port, a small enough reward after a long commission and so much achieved.

Richard was granted three weeks' leave. He took coach to London on Admiralty business and then went back to Cornwall. He had been away from home for three years, and after the dark forests and windy coasts of Nova Scotia, the lush green of the Roseland would seem especially beautiful.

Little had changed at St. Anthony, for the effects of the war had been small in that part of Cornwall. There had been the usual scares of invasion, and much excitement at the time of Charles Edward Stuart's landing in Scotland the year before. Many Cornish squires were Tories and were suspected of favouring the Stuart cause, although the Boscawens had raised thousands of men in support of King George. There had been some hardship due to interference by French privateers with the fishing and the coastwise trade. And Richard would be made aware of the growing strength of John Wesley's following among the country people, with Methodist preaching houses appearing in all manner of places. But in general life had flowed on in its usual quiet fashion, certainly very different from the hard and dangerous one he had just left.

Richard was now aged thirty-one, a personable young fellow and with enough money to buy himself an estate in Cornwall. He might have been expected to marry, for there were plenty of comely young heiresses around Cornwall, or at Plymouth. But he showed no sign of doing so. It was an age when marriage was a business rather than a romantic arrangement, and perhaps he never met anyone for whom he thought it was worth sacrificing the advantages of a single life.

Certainly he showed from time to time his interest in the opposite sex, with his mention in letters of pretty girls seen aboard a French dogger, or of buying presents to take home for a fair lady[1]. It may be that he made other arrangements, for it was not unknown for

[1] See page 125.

naval captains to keep a mistress. There were many, like Admiral John Jervis, who thought that an officer who married was lost to the navy.

More than likely Richard felt that a man who was away from home for three years at a time, had no business to rush into domesticity. Moreover, the rest of his family showed little inclination that way. His brother Arthur was still single, and sisters Charity and Lucy were spinsters. Only Mary had married, to Thomas Davey, Esquire, a landowner in St. Just in Roseland. Meanwhile Richard had little time to consider the matter deeply, for by the middle of February 1747 he was back aboard the "Chester" at Plymouth, preparing for sea.

# CHAPTER VI

## H.M.S. "CHESTER" IN SOUNDINGS

For the early months of 1747 life for Richard Spry was largely concerned with the day to day running of the ship. With the vessel just out of the dockyard after its refit, and its crew brought back from leave, or the various hulks and guard ships into which they had been distributed, most of his orders and letters are concerned with obtaining food and naval stores. She was to be provisioned with several months supply "of all Species except beer, of which you are to carry as much as she can conveniently stow".

The task of taking in victuals to feed over a long period three hundred and fifty men was the particular pre-occupation of the purser and his mates. Each mess received a daily issue of one pound of bread, and a gallon of beer per man. The rest of the diet was a monotonous round of salt beef (two pounds per man) or salt pork (one pound per man) for five days a week, relieved on non-meat or "banian" days by salt fish and cheese. Vegetables consisted of dried peas or beans or rice, with oatmeal, potatoes and various substitutes such as raisins and currants issued on a regular scale as well as small additions of sugar, butter and cocoa. The hand who had been appointed "cook of the mess" for the week drew the issue for his messmates, prepared the meal, and took it to the galley to be cooked by the ship's cooks.

The quantity of food would have been adequate - even though the hands often messed "six upon four", that is six men would only be provided with the rations of four. The quantity was comparatively generous, for the same men ashore would probably have subsisted on dry bread and cheese, and tasted meat only once a week. It was the quality that was so appalling. The "bread" was a biscuit, a mixture of wheaten and pease flour and water, made into four ounce squares in the royal dockyards. When it was fresh it was like rock, but in time it bred a soft, black headed maggot or weevil. Each man had his own way of facing the weevils. One was to eat them with the eyes shut, another was to wait until it was dark enough not to see what was being eaten.

68

The meat was salty, grisly and often had a large proportion of bone and fat. Since the oldest meat was eaten first, it had generally been pickled in the cask for years, and was so hard that even after soaking it was often inedible.

Richard and his fellow captains were well enough aware of the poor quality of the food. Many of them made repeated efforts to obtain fresh meat from the shore, and whenever possible live bullocks and sheep were brought off to be slaughtered on board. Again and agains captain's letters go to the senior officers with requests for surveys to be made on the meat, bread, cheese, butter or beer, generally described as "rotten, stinking and not fit for men to eat." These surveys commonly took the form of a visit from the masters of three other vessels, who having inspected the offending victals would decide whether they should be thrown over the side, or sent back into store.

Such a diet created thirsts that would not readily be slaked by the water, which went green and putrid after only a short time in the cask. Hence the provision of a gallon of beer per man each day. This was carried in great barrels, stowed in the bottom of the hold, and issued at dinner. When that had gone, wine would be substituted. It was generally poor stuff and to supplement it there was an issue of spirits, sometimes malt spirit, sometimes arrack, but generally rum, a gill at noon and another gill at supper time.

Drunkenness is generally recognised as having been the prime vice of all classes in the eighteenth century. The rich had their claret and port, sherry, madeira and brandy. On shore, the poor drank porter and gin in vast quantities. At sea they drank their beer and rum, both considered patriotic drinks for one helped the farmer at home, and the other the planter in the West Indies. There can be little doubt that for many men on the lower deck of His Majesty's ships the daily dram was the only thing that made life bearable.

When Richard first went to sea the spirits had been issued and drunk neat, sometimes with dire results. Drunkenness was frowned on by the service, and, if clearly intoxicated, a sailor could be flogged for it. Nevertheless, after dinner or supper men were often so drunk that accidents were common. They fell down hatches, or from aloft, or crashed their skulls on low deck beams.

The folly of this was recognised by many captains, and in 1740 Admiral Vernon, generally known as 'Old Grog' from his habit of wearing a grogram cloak, had issued his famous directive. Because "the pernicious custom of the seamen drinking their allowance in drams, and often at once, is attended with many fatal effects to their morals, which are visibly impaired thereby, and many of their lives shortened", ...... he therefore decreed that the daily half pint of rum should be mixed with a quart of water. It was the beginning of "grog", although not the end of drunkenness, for as in so much else, orders were not always carried out.

When the crew came to be mustered after the refit, Richard had the satisfaction of knowing that most of the men who had been trusted with ten days leave, had returned to the ship. Not all of course, there were always one or two who would risk hanging, and go absent. One or two others sought legal means of getting out. Thus there was Richard Pittman "born a Butcher, Farmer and Hop Planter at Bassingstke". Pittman had begged that he might be allowed to go home and help his mother in the family business. He was given a fortnight's leave and at the end of it failed to return, but instead sent letters from his local clergyman and a surgeon to say that he had been sick. Meanwhile he approached the Admiralty for a discharge, offering to provide an able seaman in his place. His request was granted.

An even more interesting case was that of John Peacock, a seaman aboard the "Chester", whose story was set out in a petition to the Admiralty and which is worth quoting at length.

> ....."In the Year 1741 he was master of the "Friend's Love" of Scarborough, George Widgate owner, and then imploy'd in the Cole trade and had the missfortune of loosing the said Vessle on the Cockles, that as he (after the said Vessell was lost) was proceeding by Land to London abot. his affairs and having then none of his Papers about him (they being lost) was imprest by Lieutenant Lang and sent on board His Majesty's Ship 'Medway', that he was afterwards turned over on board the 'Squirrel', and from thence to the 'Dolphin', and after that on board His Majesty's Ship under your Command, where he has continued ever since, that having Lately had a Ticket of Leave for ten Days ..... he went to London where meeting with a Vessell of a moderate Price, thinking thereby to advance himself in the World according bought her and therefore prays for his Discharge upon finding an Able Body'd Seaman to serve in his room."

One cannot but admire the faith and tenacity of John Peacock who, having served for seven long years on the lower deck, had managed to save enough money to buy himself a ship and his freedom. Richard agreed that his request should be granted, and the incident shows that harsh as it was, "pressing" had its humane side.

From all the cares of fitting out Richard was relieved to get an order to take aboard sixty marines and to sail for the Downs at the end of February. The trip was a quick one, for he found the "Chester" to be in excellent sailing trim. This encouraged him to ask permission from Commodore Matthew Michell, who was in charge of the vessels in the Downs, to go on a cruise off Cap Le Havre to seek out two French privateers that had been reported hovering there. The request was refused, and he was ordered to anchor off the port of Deal.

The Downs is the name given by seamen to that great anchorage lying in the lee of the land between the North and South Forelands on one side, and the Goodwin Sands on the other. It was of immense importance in the days of sail, being the meeting place for shipping bound in or out of London River, as well as for the ports of the North Sea and the Baltic. Here vessels came for shelter, to await a tide, or to collect orders. At times there would be several hundred ships lying at anchor there. To service this shipping, ferrying out stores or passengers, bringing pilots or letters or extra anchors, the men of Deal and Ramsgate maintained a large fleet of galley punts and luggers. However, such a concourse of shipping offered rich prizes to privateers from Dunkirk, who could slip over at night to cut out a merchantman, and the protection of the Downs was one of the duties of the Channel fleet.

But the Navy had other responsibilities also. The freedom of the River Schelde and the Low Countries that surround it, had been major concern of English foreign policy for centuries. Now that freedom was being attacked by French armies which had invaded Flanders. The Navy's part in the struggle was to convoy troops and supplies to aid the Dutch, and Richard was soon in the centre of these activities.

Commodore Michell moved his flag aboard H.M.S. "Chester". The Orders from him, which came thick and fast, cast an interesting light on the Navy's work. The "Chester" was required to send boarding parties aboard any vessel coming in from sea and impress as many men as they could. She was to keep aboard a number of pilots for such ships as should need them. She was to provide a petty officer and twelve armed men to patrol the anchorage in case of attack from small French fishing boats. Captain Spry was required to send the commodore an account of all vessels entering or leaving the anchorage. He was to see that three English privateers lying at anchor did not sail without permission.

Any hopes for cruise seemed a long way off, but on the twelfth of March Richard was delighted to receive orders from his old friend Rear Admiral Warren, instructing him to store his ship for a six month voyage, in preparation for joining him in a foreign commission. Deal was not the easiest place to obtain all that was needed, but Richard set about the task with his usual vigour. On the sixteenth of March he wrote to Warren saying that he would join him in Portsmouth as soon as the weather eased, and that he would bring with him three Deal cutters for the squadron.

Later that day, however, there occurred an incident that was to have a profound effect on Richard's future. Ship's business required that he should go ashore, and he set off in his six oared gig. The weather had been blowing hard from the south for days, and a long swell was running round the South Foreland, and crashing on to the beach at Deal. Landing in surf is always a difficult manoeuvre, for it is impossible to judge the height of the waves from seaward. As they approached the beach an enormous breaker picked up the gig and hurled it forward. The bow struck in the shallows, and the boat rolled over on top of her crew. Out of the confusion of arms, legs and oars, only Richard failed to get clear. He was pinned down in the surf with the boat's gunwale across his back.

Some minutes passed before the boat's crew was able to get him out, minutes in which he was dragged about in the backwash, being ground into the shingle by the heavy boat. When at last he was pulled clear, he was taken back aboard the "Chester" more than half dead, and for a time the ship's surgeon, considered he was unlikely to recover. His back and chest were so violently bruised and he had such difficulty with his breathing that it was believed he might have suffered internal injury. They strapped him up and put him to bed where he lay for the next ten days in a comatose condition.

On the twenty-eighth of March fresh orders came. The "Chester" was to proceed to Portsmouth to join a squadron under Admiral Anson. The surgeon tried to persuade Richard to stay ashore, but he had seen enough of the Downs. "I shall not presume to stay behind but shall Proceed in the ship at all Risques," he wrote valiantly. Two days later the "Chester" was anchored at Spithead, joining a powerful fleet of eighteen ships of the line, with an assortment of sloops and fireships all under the flag of George Anson.

It is easy to understand why Richard Spry, sick man though he was should be anxious to serve in that fleet. No ambitious young captain would have sought otherwise, for George Anson was not only the outstanding seaman, of his time, but had made a name for himself as a steadfast and courageous leader. The story of his voyage round the world is well known, but it is worth repeating here, for it had become a part of naval tradition, even in Richard's time.

With nearly two thousand men, H.M.S. "Centurion", of sixty guns, five smaller men of war, and two supply vessels, Anson had set out for a raiding voyage to the South Seas in 1740[1]. Four years later he returned with only the "Centurion", and two hundred men, the others having been lost or driven back on the way. Nevertheless the voyage had proved a spectacular success. Anson had beat to the westward around Cape Horn, and had carried the flag to the Far East. In the course of this cruise he had taken much wealth from the Spanish possessions in the Pacific, and had captured the Manilla galleon with a vast treasure. He brought home stores of gold and silver that at today's valuation would be in the region of fifty million pounds.

More than that, the circumnavigation had shown that in spite of the Navy's decline in the early part of the eighteenth century, British seamen could still display skill and courage in the face of endless difficulties and dangers. This knowledge was largely responsible for the surge in the morale of the naval service that became apparent in the middle of that century.

Anson had now been given another important assignment. Early in 1747 the Admiralty had learned that a considerable fleet of warships and merchantmen was being assembed by the French at Brest, and was intended as a reinforcement for their colonies in both the East and West Indies. It would be Anson's task to seek out and destroy this fleet wherever he might find it.

Vice-Admiral Anson was the ideal commander for such an expedition. In addition to his personal ability, and his enterprise and steadiness in action he was now able to display his quality as an organiser. Obviously the essential part of an admiral's task was first to find the enemy's ships, and then to manoeuvre his own fleet into the best position for falling on them. To guide him in the way he should proceed, he was issued with a list of "Fighting Instructions" which had been in

[1] See page 32.

use from the previous century. But these had tended to produce a stereo-typed series of tactics, the general aim of which was to attack in line ahead, van to enemy's van, on roughly parallel or converging courses, with the flagship directing operations from the centre of the line.

Such an aim was often difficult to achieve in the confusion and gunsmoke of an action, with shifts in the wind, masts and spars falling, and vessels not under command through loss of sails or steering gear, but it had the advantage of preventing ships from firing into vessels of their own fleet. However, by the middle of the eighteenth century, efforts to maintain this line of attack had become so fixed that battles were lost because an admiral was unable to take advantage of a changing situation, or because the captains failed to understand his intentions[1].

To make certain that this would not happen in his fleet, it was Anson's practice while the ships lay in Spithead to call the captains aboard H.M.S. "Prince George" where they could discuss his tactics, for as well as those in general use, he issued his own Additional Fighting Instructions. Spry was now joined in company with many of the ablest commanders of his day. Some of course, he knew already. Rear Admiral Peter Warren was there, flying his flag aboard H.M.S. "Devonshire", and in charge of one half of the battle line. Richard's fellow Cornishman, the Honourable Edward Boscawen, was also there in command of H.M.S. "Namur", a vessel in which he would later perform oustanding service.

But among the many younger captains Richard now met were some rising stars such as Peter Denis and Philip Saumarez, who had been with Anson on his world encircling voyage. Saumarez was a particularly attractive character. He came of a distinguished naval family from Guernsey, and had served as first lieutenant aboard the "Centurion" in the Pacific. His zeal and ability there had played a large part in the success of the voyage. He was a sensitive, gifted man completely devoted to the service, and in the previous year had distinguished himself in his ship H.M.S. "Nottingham" by the capture of the "Mars" a big French man o' war. He seemed destined to rise to the top of his profession but was to be killed later that year in Hawke's victory off Finisterre.[2]

---

[1] Anson and Hawke broke free from this restriction, as did many later admirals, such as Howe, Rodney and Nelson.

[2] Saumarez died aboard the "Nottingham" in a desperate attempt to prevent the escape of two French battleships.

Perhaps less attractive, but equally able, was Captain George Brydges Rodney of H.M.S. "Eagle". He also was of a distinguished service and aristocratic background. He made an elegant and handsome figure, although his portrait shows him to be somewhat long of nose and petulant of mouth. Rodney had joined the service in the same year as Richard. He was four years younger, but thanks to his influential connections his progress had been rapid, and he was made a captain at twenty-three. He was an arrogant young man, somewhat given to argument and free alike with his censure and praise. He had many of the eighteenth century vices, was very extravagant, and reputed to be overfond of women and gambling.

These were characteristics that were hardly likely to endear Rodney to his fellows or the men who served under him. In spite of that, as a captain he showed great skill and courage, and only a few months earlier had captured two French privateers off the Irish coast. In time he would become one of the most famous of British admirals, and prove to be a tactician of genius;- in which field it was claimed "none were his superiors and but few his equals". He would earn his country's gratitude during the dark days of the American War, and notably in 1782 at the battle of the Saints when he won one of the most memorable of naval victories against the French.

Meanwhile Richard Spry, who had much contact with him, found Rodney to be an equable enough companion. In deed he discovered this to be true of most of the captains he met in the Admiral's cabin aboard the "Prince George". These young men had much in common. They were almost all the sons of landed gentry, and most of them had entered the Navy at a very early age. There they had suffered what today would be regarded as a hard life, and all had taken part in violent action against the enemy. Such a background, and such experiences, produced in them an estimate of their own worth that bordered on conceit. They knew that in war time at least, they were their country's heroes, for Anson's voyage, the victory at Louisbourg, as well as many individual ship actions, had brought the navy immense popularity throughout Britain. Above all, these captains had no doubts about their ability to deal with other nations at sea, particularly the French and Spaniards.

France was the richest and most powerful nation in Europe at that time, having dominated politics on the Continent for over a hundred years. French abilities as workers and craftsmen, soldiers and navigators were well recognised in Britain. Yet their seamen were often dismissed by Richard Spry and his fellows somewhat contempuously, as "gasconading chaps" and "troublesome rascals"; while as regards their ships, they said, "The French to build 'em, the English to sail them". Peter Warren summed it up when he wrote to Anson.

> "I can't help thinking that we have this advantage over them (i.e. the French) that our Officers are better Seamen than theirs, and I hope as Valiant, and our Men in general more Robust and Stronger, and never were thought to want courage, - tho' they have very little virtue of any other kind".

That final comment, which rather takes the gilt off the previous remarks is revealing, and typical of 18th century attitudes. For while the bravery of Jack Tar in his natural element was applauded in ballad and legend, in other respects he was held in very low opinion. While Anson's captains sat sipping the admiral's madeira in his magnificent cabin, they were well aware that the men on whom they depended to work the ships and fight the guns, were living but a few yards away in vile conditions. They did not approve of the fact that their crews were worm-fed, cheated and hard-driven, but generally accepted it as the natural order of things. As we have seen, many captains were concerned to do what they could for the health and well being of their men, but they did not believe the system could be easily altered. Admiral Vernon was one of the few who spoke out. He said that "our fleets are defrauded by injustice, manned by violence and maintained by cruelty," and for that he was dismissed from the service. It would be nearly a hundred years before such grievances were remedied. Meanwhile, in Anson's fleet morale was high among the officers as they planned and prepared for the campaign ahead of them.

Anson got his ships away from Portsmouth on April the sixth, and after a brief call at Plymouth proceeded into the Bay of Biscay. Off the Isles of Scilly they took a French privateer, the "Mary Magdalen", which had been a considerable nuisance in these waters having already captured fifteen British merchantmen. Otherwise they saw nothing of the enemy. However Anson had a fairly exact knowledge of the French intentions, and he took up station to the west of Finisterre, confident that they would pass that way. For nearly a month his fleet cruised, practising manoeuvres and exercising in gunnery and signals.

It had always been difficult for an admiral to make clear his intentions at sea. There was a book of general signalling instructions, supplemented by private signals issued by the admiral to his captains. At night lanterns would be displayed, and by day coloured flags would be hoisted, in various parts of the flagship's rigging. In fine weather a boat could be sent, or a speaking trumpet used at close quarters. But in general, signalling was a clumsy procedure, and led to frequent misunderstanding.[1] It also involved H.M.S. "Chester" in a series of misfortunes.

Throughout the weeks at sea, Richard had carried on his duties aboard the "Chester", although greatly troubled by the injuries he had received in the Downs. On the thirteenth of April he was called over to the flagship, - the signal being a red pendant hoisted at the starboard side of the main yard arm. He was required to carry instructions to Captain Saumarez, who was some considerable distance away. The wind was blowing hard, and perhaps Richard was too anxious. For while "Chester" was beating towards the "Nottingham" he carried away his main topmast, which in falling brought down a number of other spars. The work of clearing the wreckage and sending up a new topmast occupied all hands until nightfall, and then Richard being exhausted and in some pain, retired to his bed. Except in special circumstances a captain did not keep a watch at night.

About midnight he was wakened by the master, who had charge of the watch, to say that lanterns had been shown aboard the flagship requiring the fleet to tack. Richard recalled that when he went to sleep all the ships had been hove to, and therefore concluded the signal could only have meant that they should get under way again. He instructed the master to do so, but presently that officer came again to say that two ships were passing close-by, and tacking to the northward. Richard therefore ordered him to follow them and keep them in sight. But when dawn came he discovered that the "Chester" had been trailing an English merchant ship, and that in company with the fireship H.M.S. "Pluto", which had made the same error, he had lost the rest of the fleet.

For Richard staring at the wide and near-empty sea, it must have been a terrible moment. He could make excuses to himself that he was still a sick man, and that he had turned in exhausted by the mishaps of the day, but all his training told him that his failure to verify the admiral's signal reflected on him as a captain. This was one of the

---

[1] The navy had to wait another 35 years before Kempenfelt produced a series of code flags which allowed an Admiral to talk to his fleet with clearly understood signals.

penalties of command. Richard had always regarded losing contact with the fleet as an unpardonable sin, and it was made worse on this occasion by the fact that one of Anson's most recent orders had been to warn his officers against it.

He took H.M.S. "Pluto" under his command, and with the wind at north west they made their way to the north eastward hoping that every distant sail might prove to be one of Anson's fleet. Unfortunately, at that time Anson was on the opposite tack, sailing towards the south west. H.M.S. "Chester" and "Pluto" searched an empty sea unsuccessfully for a week and then had the good fortune to fall in with a squadron of six English ships, led by Captain Fox in H.M.S. "Kent". These vessels, which included Rodney in the "Eagle", had sailed from England three days after Anson, and had failed to find him at any of the appointed rendezvous. That they had been vainly searching for nearly a month is another indication of how vast the sea could be in the days of sail.

Richard placed himself under Fox's orders, and they continued to cruise, looking for their admiral. They were quite unaware, that Anson had in fact caught the French fleet three days before. That fleet had consisted of five battle ships and five frigates, protecting twenty eight merchantmen, and although the French had fought valiantly they had been overwhelmed by Anson's superior force. Eighteen prizes were taken without the loss of any British ships, this being the first truly decisive naval battle of the war. Anson had thereupon returned to England, soon to be rewarded with the title of Lord Anson, while Rear Admiral Warren was knighted.

Meanwhile, Captain Fox and his squadron continued to search about the Bay of Biscay until mid-June. At last the news from Anson was brought to them, and they turned for England. A few days later however they came upon a huge homeward bound convoy, a hundred and thirty four French merchantmen, sailing from San Domingo with only three men or war to protect them. This vast fleet was sighted early in the morning, and the British squadron went after them like hounds let loose. But the wind was light northerly, and for a time it seemed they might lose their quarry in fog. They found them again just before dark. The convoy now scattered, one half fleeing to the westward, the others turning east. The British ships pursued the latter half, just keeping in touch through the faint light of the midsummer night.

The next morning with the weather still calm they could only take one prize, but on the following day the score rose to thirteen. The day after, it was now twenty-third of June, a south westerly gale sprang up but in spite of that another thirty four vessels were captured.

Somewhat glutted, and now short of hands to man their forty-eight prizes, Fox and his squadron returned to England. It had been a highly successful adventure, and each captain had made himself a considerable fortune in prize money. Richard Spry's share alone, was to come to £8,165-1-0d!

On his return to Portsmouth, Richard was faced with the unpleasant business of writing to Vice Admiral Anson to explain how H.M.S. "Chester" had lost contact with his fleet, and so missed the battle. The subsequent success under Fox must have made this a little easier, nevertheless Richard's letter shows something of the agony of spirit he had suffered. Having congratulated Anson on his victory - which he described as "an Action that will make your name Revered by every good Englishman to the latest Posterity", he went on to explain how he lost the fleet, and to express his remorse.

> "I can justly say I have suffered more Uneasiness on this Occasion than anything I ever met with since I have been in the Service, as it must consequently give you an ill Opinion of me, it being the first time I ever had the Honour of being in a Fleet under your Command."

Anson was noted for his generous spirit and he could afford to be particularly magnanimous on this occasion. His reply to Richard, taciturn as ever, approved of his subsequent conduct, and as a further mark of trust, put him in charge of seventeen of the prizes which were to be taken round to the Thames.

The "Chester" sailed for the Downs, where the prizes would take aboard pilots for London river and thereafter proceed independently. To Richard's astonishment on their arrival, on a fine day with a fair wind and a flowing tide, the largest and most valuable ship in the company, the "Saint Esprit", was sailed straight on to the Goodwin Sands "due to the Ignorance and Wilfulness of the Pilot."

There followed moments of drama. Richard called away the "Chester's" boats and boarded the stranded vessel. As the tide had begun to ebb they carried out anchors, and removed casks of indigo to lighten her. The weather remained quiet and there was every hope that she might be refloated when the tide rose again. But the Goodwin Sands are notoriously cruel to stranded ships. When the flood tide began, the current sucked the sand from beneath the "Saint Esprit's" bilge, so that she fell over on her beam-ends, and began to take in water. By now Richard had commandeered boats from Deal, and was landing cargo as quickly as he could. After dark he had gone back aboard the "Chester", when the local wreckers arrived, bringing their boats from Ramsgate. They cut the cables that were holding the "Saint Esprit" and began to strip her of everything of value. Legally she was not yet a wreck, and hearing the disturbance Richard returned with an armed boat's crew, soon to be joined by Captain Rodney from H.M.S. "Eagle". This involved them in a spirited confrontation, which ended with fifty of the wreckers finding themselves pressed into the Service.

It was a bold action on the part of the two captains, for the long-shoremen of Kent were not only a wild lot, but considered themselves to be free of impressment as a recognition of their importance to shipping generally. Spry and Rodney were now assailed from Ramsgate with requests for the release of the prisoners, and to forestall this, Rodney sailed for Plymouth taking all but a dozen of them with him. Spry left with the remainder solved the difficulty in a practical manner, as he explained to the Admiralty. Five of the men were to be released,

> "being represented by a number of Gentlemen as Masters of their own Business and with very great Families which must inevitably starve if they were taken from them, I thought it for the Good of His Majesty's Service to discharge these, on their friends producing an able seamen in the room of each of them, the other seven are all stout Young Fellows whom I have kept on board."

This rough justice seemed to satisfy all but the victims, and the final result was that His Majesty's Service gained fifty able, if not altogether willing seamen, and Ramsgate lost a number of lawless characters.

For the remainder of that summer H.M.S. "Chester" was busily engaged in convoy work along the south coast, and carrying supplies to the British expeditionary force on the island of Walcheren. It was an arduous business conducted in an area of shallow waters and strong tides, and Richard was glad at last to get orders which took him back to Plymouth. There he was directed to serve under Boscawen and prepare for a long voyage in tropical waters.

# CHAPTER VII

## A PASSAGE TO PONDICHERRY

The Honourable Edward Boscawen, recently promoted to rear admiral was well known to Richard.[1] He had earned for himself a considerable reputation in the navy, for although only a few years older than Richard he had seen a deal of varied action since the age of fourteen. He had particularly distinguished himself in the early part of the war then in progress when, in command of a small sloop H.M.S. "Shoreham", he had led a spirited attack on the Spanish batteries at Cartagena. In 1744 he had captured a French frigate, the "Medée", now renamed H.M.S. "Boscawen" in his honour. Above all, in Anson's recent victory off Finisterre he had increased his fame by leading the attack on the enemy fleet. When the Admiral had flown the signal for a "General Chase", Boscawen's ship the "Namur", being a better sailer than the rest had fought single handed against the French line, until others could come up - "by which daring but judicious manoeuvre he principally contributed to the success with which the English arms were crowned".

In the action that followed, the "Namur" had been much damaged and Boscawen severely wounded in the shoulder, in spite of which he took the surrender of two French men-of-war, the "Serieux" and the "Ruby". Largely as a result of this success had come his recent promotion to flag rank, and his new appointment as commander of both land and sea forces on an expedition to India.

The British and French had been trading rivals in the Far East for over a hundred years. Their respective East India Companies had received concessions from various princes, and each had built forts and factories on the coasts, but hitherto with little thought of establishing territorial empires. The rewards of enterprise had been considerable however and the ships of both companies brought large and valuable cargoes of tea, porcelain, silks and spices to London and Lorient. Now

---

[1] The Boscawens of Tregothnan were near neighbours in Cornwall. They owned property in the Roseland, including the sea-mill at Place, leased from them by the Sprys.

the French company under their able and energetic Commandant General Dupleix had taken the offensive, seeing the present war as an opportunity to drive the British out of India altogether. He seemed set to suceed in this with his capture in 1746 of the important British factory at Madras, although Anson's victory off Finisterre had spoiled his plans somewhat. Part of the captured convoy had been carrying troops and stores for Dupleix, and among papers then taken had been found French plans for strengthening their position in India. Boscawen's expedition was now formed to counter those intentions by seizing their chief fort at Pondicherry.

Spry's early letters to his new commander in chief follow the usual pattern. There are the normal complaints of the difficulty in getting work completed in the dockyard at Plymouth and the shortage of seamen. Even recruiting expeditions sent into his home land of Cornwall had failed to produce many men. But finally in early September he was able to write that he needed only to get spare topmasts, yards and boats, aboard and he would be able to join the fleet at Portsmouth. Amid all the problems of getting his own vessel repaired, and mustering ships and men, the admiral still found time to write friendly letters in reply. He expresses pleasure at having Richard under his command, gives him a week's leave in London, asks him to take as a rated servant "the son of a Cornish friend of mine (Mr. Truscott of St. Stephens)", and requests he would bring with him a new Deal cutter with oars, masts and sails that he had left behind in Plymouth.

The fleet that Richard joined at Spithead in mid September 1747 was an impressive one. There were six ships of the line, and several smaller naval vessels. There were in addition fourteen large armed vessels of the East India Company, carrying troops and military stores. This was an important expedition for it was the largest Britain had ever sent to the Far East. Boscawen's appointment was also an unusual one in that he was not only in supreme command of the ships with their eight hundred marines, but also of the East India Company's army of fifteen hundred soldiers.

There can be no doubt of the soundness of the choice of Boscawen as the leader of this force, a choice inspired by Anson who was now at the Admiralty. He had the required qualities of an aristocratic backgrounds, much sea experience, and a strong personality. He had also some fame as a disciplinarian, of officers as well as seamen. The lower deck loved him, speaking of him, behind his back, as "Old Dreadnought". This later became "Wry-necked Dick", from his habit of standing with his head on one side[1].

Boscawen was also well in advance of his time in his concern for the health and well being of his crew, taking care to provide fresh meat and vegetables wherever possible[2]. On the forthcoming voyage to India he was to adopt the use of "windsails" or canvas ventilators, to carry much needed air below hatches, and years later he would take the lead in advocating better leave for the seamen in home ports, prompted no doubt by an incident that happened aboard H.M.S. "Namur" in 1747, shortly after the victory off Finisterre.

It was one of the intolerable injustices of the naval service that during war time shore leave was rarely granted to the men of the lower deck in home ports. Captains were often forbidden to permit any leave at all, for fear that the crew would run. Instead the men were granted a concession that women, their so-called "wives", were allowed to live on board. One of the usual scenes when one of His Majesty's vessels came to anchor was the arrival of "bum boats" alongside, bringing the young women of the town, ready to strike a bargain, and move in with their fancy man until the ship sailed. Since the girls often brought concealed supplies of liquor, the mess deck would then become a scene of wild revelry. Aboard "Namur" on this occasion it got out of hand. Some of the men seized arms and demanded to be allowed ashore. But the officers and leading hands contained the rebels below decks, until help came from other ships. The mutiny was all over in a couple of hours, and there was very little bloodshed, although in the typical savage justice of the time, three men were later hanged, and another dozen sentenced to be flogged around the fleet.

Boscawen was not involved in this incident, for he had been put ashore wounded. Although he would go along with the strict punishment, it was the nature of the man to do what he could later to remove the cause of the trouble. Meanwhile, many of the orders to Spry when he joined the fleet stressed the need to keep a tight grip on his crew, and to make sure that no one was ever allowed ashore after dark.

There were inevitable delays in getting so large a body of ships to sea. Before they sailed there came news of a second great victory off Finisterre. Peter Warren who was now in command of the Western

[1] Probably the result of the neck wound he received at Finisterre.
[2] When commanding a blockading fleet of Quiberon he took possession of one of the islands in the Morbihan to grow green vegetables for the use of the sick men aboard his ships.

Squadron had been taken ill, and his place filled by Rear Admiral Hawke. The French were making another attempt to reinforce their possessions in the West Indies, and Hawke intercepted a large convoy in the Bay of Biscay. He followed Anson's tactics in ordering a General Chase with the result that six ships were taken[1]. Richard learned with pleasure that his old ally George Rodney had played a brilliant part in the success of the action, a pleasure dimmed by the news of the death of Philip Saumarez.

Boscawen finally got his fleet to sea on the fourth of November, leading the way in his old flagship H.M.S. "Namur". The "Namur" was one of the famous vessels of her day, having been built as a Second Rate of 90 guns, in 1729; and had taken part in many actions in the Mediterranean and the Western Approaches. To Richard she was a familiar sight indeed, for his memories of her went back to his own first voyages in the navy. He had been in her company time and again at Lisbon in 1735, at Port Mahon in the early days of the war, as well as during Anson's cruise in the present year. She had been cut down lately to a Third Rate of 74 guns, but was still a fine, fast, hard-hitting vessel setting an enormous spread of canvas.

The fleet soon ran into difficulties. The wind blew stormily from the westward and even after six days of beating to and fro across the Channel they had failed to weather Start Point. Boscawen decided to anchor in Torbay, but as they were about to do so suddenly the wind shifted to the north west, and they were on their way again.

Their passage south, some $10^0$W to avoid the Bay of Biscay in winter, went well, except for the inevitable irritation of the naval captains with some of their merchant ship colleagues. The East India Company's ships were fine vessels, well maintained and well run. Some indeed were like men-of-war in appearance and organisation, with ex-naval lieutenants among their officers. But in others there were strong individualists in command who did not take kindly to sailing in convoy, with all the difficulties of station keeping and the need to obey signals. On the nineteenth of November the "Chester" received an order from the "Namur".

> "As I observe the India Ships do not pay due regard to
> my signals and especially with respect to bearing down
> into my Wake before Night, which must greatly

---

[1] Most of the convoy escaped during the night, but due to a warning sent by Hawke to Commodore Pocock, they were captured before they reached the Caribbean.

hazard their loossing Company, You are hereby
required and directed whenever I make a signal for the
future, and you Perceive any who happen to be near
you not to obey it, immediately to fire a Shot at them
and continue doing so until they Comply."

In spite of these difficulties at the end of the month the fleet
arrived safely at Madeira and anchored in Funchal Roads. Here they lay
for several weeks, taking the opportunity of stocking up with wine and
fruit.

They sailed again at the beginning of January 1748 and almost at
once met with more trouble. Due to what Richard called "an
Unavoidable Accident", which we can only conclude was bad weather,
the fleet was scattered. Richard found himself as Senior Officer of a
small squadron consisting of the hospital ship "Apollo", His Majesty's
Bomb "Basilisk", and six of the Indiamen. He shepherded this little
flock on to the next rendezvous which was at Porto Praya in the Cape
Verde Islands, where he was relieved to find the rest of the fleet at
anchor.

They weighed again at the end of the month, starting on a long
slow voyage which took them through the last of the N.E. Trades, then
drifting through the oily calms of the Doldrums, to cross the Equator in
longitude $28^0$ West; thus bringing them well towards the coasts of
Brazil. They picked up the wind again a few degrees south of the
Equator, making a brisk passage close hauled in the S.E. Trades until
they crossed the meridian of Greenwich once more, in latitude $36^0$
South. Now they steered eastwards in the Anti-Trades until the tip of
Africa was brought to the north east of them, when they made straight
for Cape Town. It was a roundabout passage, but was already well
established as the sailing ship route down the south Atlantic, and was
familiar to the men of the East India Company ships.

They had been nearly two months at sea, and now there was to be
a long spell in Table Bay providing a pleasant interlude. Cape Town had
been a staging post for voyagers to the East ever since Drake's time. The
climate was a splendid one, although seamen were well aware of how its
weather could be subject to sudden change, from sunny calm one
minute to heavy rain and a snorting south easter the next. But Richard
had been provided with detailed sailing directions for the Bay, and
anchored the "Chester" with the rest of the fleet well up on the weather
shore.

*H.M.S. "Namur". A Third Rate of 74 guns*

Nearly a hundred years earlier the Dutch West Africa Company had founded a prosperous colony here. They built a fortress and a pier protecting the landing places. Outside the citadel there were long straight streets of houses and gardens, and beyond these on the lower slopes of Table Mountain, farms which raised fine herds of sheep and oxen. The settlers grew vegetables; peas, beans and salads to supply the seafarers, and their vineyards of Groot Constantia had already achieved well deserved fame among seamen.

Now there was fresh meat for all hands, with rations increased to a pound and a half of beef or mutton each day. The troops were landed and put into camps. Shore leave was given to the seamen, although inevitably this caused trouble. After months of being cooped up in their ships, hundreds of sailors went searching for drink and women. Such were their "Disorders and Violences" that they were restricted to certain parts of the town, in particular being forbidden to go near the Dutch Company's slave houses.

More ships continued to arrive, including a number of Dutch Indiamen carrying troops. At last early in May, the soldiers were brought back aboard and the fleet put to sea again with orders to attack the French islands of the Mauritius group. These lay nearly three thousand miles to the eastward of Cape Town, and thus athwart the route to India. They were used as a base by French privateers which would lie in wait for merchant ships bound for the Orient, and clearly the seizure of such islands would be a major success for Britain.

The fleet arrived off Mauritius on the twenty-third of June, where they anchored in Turtle Bay, a few miles to the north of the capital, Port Louis. But they found that the French had been forewarned, and the long delays of the voyage had given them time to erect strong defences. A French man-of-war, the "Alcide" lay across the harbour entrance in Port Louis. Heavy surf over coral reefs and beaches made landing difficult, and one attempt to do so by the ships' boats was driven off. So after a few days of indecision, a council of war aboard the "Namur" decided the risks were too great. They should proceed to their second and more important objective, the capture of Pondicherry.

After another month at sea, lumbering along before the south west monsoon they arrived at Fort St. David, the British settlement some ten miles to the south of Pondicherry. They found a British squadron under Admiral Griffin already there, for the place had been under imminent danger of attack from Dupleix.

Fort St. David was the defence point of the British East India Company's station at Cuddalore. Like most other harbours on the Coromandel coast it was an open roadstead, and the ships had to lie at anchor well clear of the surf. It was an inconvenient place, safe enough during the summer months when the wind was off shore, but all supplies had to be ferried off by specially constructed native boats. In winter the North easterly monsoon would blow on shore and then the anchorage would become untenable. For the same reason, the attack on Pondicherry now required to be pressed forward without delay. So there began the difficult operation of landing the troops through the surf, ready to make a march on the enemy by land. That done, the warships sailed northward, to anchor as close as they could off the French port.

Pondicherry, defended by a fortress within a walled town, was the chief trading centre of the French East India Company. It stood above sandy shores, guarding the entrance of a small river and lagoon. On the seaward side the town was protected by shallows, which ran out in places for nearly a mile. Monsieur Dupleix, having had plenty of notice of the danger of attack, had taken energetic action to defend the town. He had cleared the ground outside the walls of trees, had built up extra defence points and batteries, had brought in fresh troops and ample stocks of ammunition. He could await the outcome with some confidence, for he too knew that time was on his side. If he could hold out until October, the weather would force the British to retire.

At the beginning of August, the attack began. Boscawen moved his troops by land from Fort St. David and almost immediately ran into serious resistance on the south side of the river. Here a small fort named Areacopang, reported by his engineers to be of little strength, proved to be well defended, and a large number of soldiers were killed or wounded in taking it. However, he now moved across the river and surrounded the town on the North Western side. This was an area of rice fields, with streams, pools and marshes that made progress difficult. Nevertheless the troops dug trenches and built batteries, and pushed their advance works close to the town. Meanwhile the navy had been landing their nine pounder guns and ammunition. Spry had been out in the "Chester's" boats taking soundings along the shore. He reported that only to the north could the big vessels get within quarter a mile of the port, and still remain afloat. However it was decided that when all was ready the ships would move in and bombard the town.

There were many setbacks for the besiegers. In the middle of August the French made a sudden sally and captured some of the advanced British trenches. The took several prisoners among the soldiers, including their leader Major Stringer Lawrence, at the same time picking up the purser and a number of sailors from H.M.S. "Deptford" who had inadvertently gone ashore to cut wood for the galley. The trenches were soon re-captured, and French prisoners taken in turn, but although such skirmishing went on the main defences remained untouched. Now the usual sickness began among the attacking troops. The heat, the mosquitoes, the waterlogged trenches and vile quarters made this inevitable. As we have seen in other campaigns, hundreds more would die of disease than of battle.

At last, in the third week of September, Boscawen ordered the final attack. The navy moved in and began a cannonade of the defences, but they were unable to get close enough to be really effective. Their shot fell into the town, but in return they suffered much damage and many casualties from return fire. H.M.S. "Chester" had her rigging shot away, and so much damage done forward that she lost her bowsprit. The attack on land was halted, and finally the ships were pulled back out of range, having accomplished little.

A few days later the rains began. It was now apparent that Pondicherry would not be captured before the N.E. monsoon set in. More than a thousand lives had been lost by the attacking forces, and the sickness was still increasing. Richard Spry was among those who suffered. He wrote to his immediate superior, Commodore Lisle of H.M.S. "Vigilant" "I am so Excessively ill with the dry Gripes that the use of my Leggs are entirely taken from me, and am now in such Agonie that I know not what I say or do." On receipt of this, H.M.S. "Chester" was sent back to Cuddalore carrying the sick and wounded from the other ships to hospital, and with orders to lie off Fort St. David until required.

Boscawen had decided it was time to raise the siege. Guns and stores were re-embarked, the army retired down the coast to Cuddalore, and the ships sailed for Fort St. David. It was as well they did, for they shortly learned that peace had been made some months before and any further action would have meant even more useless deaths.

The campaign against Pondicherry had been a failure, though Boscawen can hardly be blamed for that. On shore he had been dependent on his army engineers, and much of their advice had been useless. Moreover he had in Dupleix and the French Company's troops, opponents whose determination and skill in warfare were equal to his own. Valuable lessons had been learned however, not least by one of the young officers in the employ of the British East India Company. This was Robert Clive, whose experiences before Pondicherry would be of value to him in later campaigns against the French.

So the war which had begun against Spain nine years before, when Vernon's victory at Portobello set the bells ringing throughout Britain, had fizzled into something of a stalemate. Both sides had suffered enough. The successes of the British navy at sea had been matched by those of the French army in Europe. So at the Treaty of Aix-la-Chapelle which ended the war, most of the territories that had been taken were exchanged. Madras went back to the British East India Company, and to the fury of the American colonists who had fought hard for it, Louisbourg was returned to France. But if no one gained or lost very much, no one was really satisfied either. The rights of trade in the West Indies which had sparked off the war were still unresolved, as were the boundaries between French and English territories in North America.

The last real battle of the war was fought half a world away from India, off the coasts of Cuba. Yet in a curious way Richard Spry was closely connected with it. His old captain, now Commodore Charles Knowles, had caught a Spanish fleet from Havana, led by Richard's benefactors, the Admirals Reggio and Spinola. Also among the Spanish forces had been the privateer "La Galga", still under his hated enemy Pedro Cochea. But that battle had been indecisive too, and although Reggio's flagship had been destroyed, Cochea and "La Galga" had escaped.

Any hopes among Boscawen's forces that the end of the war meant that they would return home was soon dispelled. Most of the ships were sent to join Admiral Griffin, who was based at Trincomalee. Ceylon was in the hands of the Dutch, and the huge and beautiful harbour provided safe and ample anchorage for the battered fleet. Here they lay surrounded by palm trees and white coral beaches, repairing damage, setting up new masts, careening, taking in stores.

They stayed in Trincomalee throughout the winter monsoon, and after some weeks discontent began to show among the ship's companies. There were grumbles about victuals, for they were required to eat rice instead of bread, and drink palm spirit, instead of rum. Grumbles turned to trouble-making. Although fresh beef was supplied from the shore, men from some of the ships took arms and went into the "King of Candye's country" driving off the villagers' buffaloes and killing them for meat.

On other occasions men from the fleet took the ships' boats and waylaid native fishermen on their way to market, and robbed them of their fish. Yet again some of them went dredging over the oyster banks in the harbour, either for a change of food, or as the Dutch governor of the port complained, "for the Lucre of a few Paltry Pearls". The governor had to make repeated complaints about such behavious to Admiral Griffin who in turn passed them on to the ships' captains with appropriate threats. The truth was that all hands were suffering from too long in harbour, a condition so well described by Joseph Conrad when he wrote: "Ports are no good, ships rot, men go to the devil."

The ships' officers used the usual methods of keeping the devil at bay. They worked the men hard for six days a week, holystoning decks, scraping, painting and tarring, and on the endless maintenance of a sailing ship's rigging. On the seventh they used the panoply of rounds, divisions and church service. Whenever possible they fired their ceremonial guns; seventeen guns for His Majesty's Birthday, fifteen for the anniversary of Gunpowder Plot, another fifteen in memory of the Duke of Cumberland's late victory at Culloden. A fine noise it made

*Admiral Sir Edward Boscawen by J. Reynolds*

with each ship firing in succession around the fleet. But without a real war to fight they faced a losing battle against sickness, mischief and boredom.

Even the captains were not quite immune. Early in January 1749 Spry wrote to Admiral Boscawen, who was then at Fort St. David. He was requesting a new main mast for the "Chester", and seeking permission to have the ship hove-down for a bottom clean. But he took the opportunity of saying,

> "I hope Sir the time I have been in this disagreeable Place, and the Number of Men I have buried here will induce you to decide in my favour, ..... I suppose you will not be much longer in India, and hope you will not leave the "Chester" behind (for I am quite tired of this vile Country)".

Poor Richard, he had been ill again, this time suffering from leg ulcers and lameness, and he was in no state to appreciate the undoubted beauty of Ceylon. He no longer took any pleasure in seeing exotic places, the ancient temples, the strange but lovely native craft. The winter rains had driven from his mind the memory of the brilliant weather of summer, and like any other sailor his thoughts continually turned homeward. He received a comforting reply from the Admiral, and a promise that when the expected orders were received to return to England, the "Chester" would not be forgotten.

Alas for such hopes. They were confounded by a disaster that struck some of the vessels which had moved up to Fort St. David in April. A late storm from the north east ravaged the whole Coromandel coast. Boscawen and some of his crew were on shore, and they were the fortunate ones. But the "Namur", and H.M.S. "Pembroke" and two merchant ships belonging to the East India Company were trapped on a lee shore. Unable to get to sea, they cut away their masts to reduce windage, but their anchors slowly dragged until all four vessels were driven into the breakers. Little could be done to help them, and in the "Namur" alone five hundred men were drowned.

With the return of settled weather in May the rest of the fleet came up from Trincomalee. The Admiral's flag was hoisted for a time aboard H.M.S. "Chester", and during this period an interesting order was promulgated by Boscawen to all ships. It had been issued by King George the year before, when the war ended. It began,

"Whereas the Rt Honourable the Lords Commis
sioners of the Admiralty have thought it Necessary the
Better to Distinguish the Rank of Sea Officers, to
Establish Military uniform Cloathing, for Admirals,
Captains, Commanders, and Lieutenants, as also that
Person acting as Midshipman, in order to their
Carrying the Appearance which is Necessary to
Distinguish their Class to be in the Rank of
Gentlemen, and to give them better Credit and Figure
in Executing the Commands of their Superior
Officers" and so on and on.

After which preamble the order established at last a naval uniform for
officers, consisting of a blue collarless coat, with white cuffs, and
embroidered according to rank. Blue breeches, white stockings,
buckled shoes and a tricorne hat completed the ensemble.

Hitherto sea officers had worn what their fancy or purse
dictated. For the wealthy it would be whatever was the contemporary
fashion, perhaps blue with gold laced edgings, or grey with scarlet
trimmings, red waistcoat and red breeches. But a poorer Lieutenant,
without hope of promotion, might have appeared in any odd and
shabby garment that he could afford.

Now all officers must wear the proper uniform at all proper
times, although for long afterwards midshipmen were notorious for
their scarecrow appearance at sea. So too were the seamen, who would
continue to wear what they could afford to buy through "slops". At its
smartest these were generally grey kersey jackets and breeches, with
blue and white chequered shirts, a striped red and white waistcoat, and a
gaily coloured handkerchief round the neck. At sea however he might
continue to wear any old and tattered garment of frieze or canvas. Not
until after the Napoleonic wars was it though necessary for Jack to wear
a uniform rig.

Throughout the summer of 1749 Boscawen's fleet stayed on the
east coast of India cruising between Fort St. David and Madras which
had now been handed back to the British East India Company. Trouble
with the hands continued. One of the "Chester's" men, Thomas Sheary
by name, stole a musket from H.M.S. "Deptford" and sold it to a native
ashore for the sum of eight rupees. When the crime was discovered and
Sheary accused, he confessed and the gun was recovered. According to
regulations he should have been court martialled, and would

undoubtedly have been hanged. But the man was so penitent and helpful that Captain Lake of the "Deptford" and Richard Spry between them decided that a flogging would be sufficient punishment. Accordingly the "Chester's" grating was rigged by the gangway, and with all the panoply that such occasions demanded — hands fallen in, marines drawn up in files, captain and officers on the quarterdeck, — Sheary received four dozen strokes of the cat o' nine tails.

This punishment was no deterrent to another of the "Chester's" seamen, Henry Drake. He stole one of the ship's boats and rowed ashore with the intention of deserting. Possibly he thought to escape to one of the East India Company's ships. But he was shortly recaptured, and after a court martial, hanged at the "Chester's" yard arm, again with all the required panoply of justice seen to be done.

To the relief of all hands, orders for home came at last. It was important that they should get off the coast before the onset of the next winter monsoon. In mid October Boscawen, now Rear Admiral of the White, hoisted his flag aboard H.M.S. "Exeter", and with a squadron of six ships of the line and four frigates, set sail for the Cape of Good Hope. They arrived in Table Bay two months later. Here Richard was required to take aboard twenty men belonging to a French East Indiaman, the "Centaur", lately cast away on the coast. The late enemies were to be treated as his own ship's company on the passage to Europe, - an interesting example of the fraternity of the sea.

The squadron sailed again at the end of January and after a short stay at St. Helena arrived at Spithead in the middle of April, 1750. Here they came under the immediate command of Vice Admiral Edward Hawke. They were to land their soldiers, and their marines, and French survivors. Ships books, store lists and pay chits had to be made up and sent to their respective offices. On the twenty-sixth of April Richard was given permission to take a fair wind for Plymouth, where the "Chester" was to be cleared of all stores, and having been unrigged, be paid off.

That was the end of Boscawen's Indian campaign, but from it there emerges a story that excited a deal of interest at the time. Among the ships that paid off at Spithead was H.M.S. "Eltham", and one member of her company, a marine named Jemmy Gray, now made a surprising disclosure. Gray, it seems, was a young women who had enlisted in Colonel Fraser's Marine Regiment at Portsmouth three years earlier. Her real name was Hannah Snell, and she claimed that as a young girl she had married a Dutch sailor. He soon deserted her, and she had spent many years wandering the country looking for him. In

1747 however she joined the marines disguised as a man and had sailed aboard His Majesty's Sloop "Swallow" as part of the fleet bound for India.

"Jemmy" had taken part in the attack on the fort at Areacopang, and her courage had earned many commendations from the officers. Later when serving in the trenches at Pondicherry she had been badly wounded, but with the help of a native woman had cured herself. She was one of those sent sick to the hospital at Cuddalore, and thereafter was drafted to H.M.S. "Eltham" for the homeward voyage.

Bearing in mind the close proximity in which life was lived aboard a man-of-war, it is difficult to believe that she maintained her disguise throughout. However she claimed that such was the case, and as a result of all her adventures was able to obtain a small pension from the Government, - "as a reward for the many signal services she did for her country." After a spell on the stage, where she appeared as "Bill Bobstay the Sailor", and sang nautical ballads, Mistress Snell went no more a-roving. Instead she opened a pub in Wapping and, under the sign of "The Widow in Masquerade, or The Female Warrior", made a new successful career.

Meanwhile H.M.S. "Chester" having also been paid off, Richard Spry was free to go home. In many ways it must have been a sad time. He had been in command of the ship for over four years, during which time he had hardly stirred out of her. She had carried him in safety from the coasts of North America to those of Africa and India. He had seen in her good times and bad, and when he left her on the fifteenth of May 1750 it can only have been with regret.

But the war was over, and in the usual fashion those who had lately been regarded as heroes now became beggars. Seamen and soldiers returned to a country that no longer needed them, and so became something of a problem. The navy was cut down to a quarter of its strength; but Richard was one of the lucky ones, for although there was no ship for him he was sent home on half pay.

The only portrait we have of him must have been painted about this time, for he appears in the recently insituted uniform. He makes a presentable enough figure, fair-haired, blue-eyed, and with a humorous quirk to his mouth. He was of course putting on weight, as most captains did, the result of large dinners, too much wine and not enough exercise.

# CHAPTER VIII

## FROM TWO FRIGATES

When Richard Spry came back to St. Anthony in the summer of 1750, he was faced with his first prolonged stay ashore for seventeen years. As on earlier occasions, he found that little had changed at home. Other parts of Cornwall had seen a vast increase in mining for tin and copper, using the new steam engines for pumping water out of deep mines. Tin was now being smelted with coal in reverberatory furnaces. Money was being poured in to mining, new men were coming in, making fortunes and setting themselves up as landed gentlemen. Fortunes had been made by some of the old families too, the Boscawens having done particularly well by leasing some of their lands for mining ventures. But none of these changes had touched the Roseland, where Richard's brother went on farming the estate in the old way. That summer of 1750 was a notably fine one, "as hot" men said, "as the weather in the Indies". In the towns people went mad with the heat, but in the Roseland they had a good hay harvest, followed by an early corn one, and after that fine hauls of pilchards. And all the time they went on raising their herds of sheep and bullocks for the markets at Tregony and Truro.

Little of this could be of interest to Richard, although he must have noted the great increase of coastal shipping in Falmouth harbour. The anchorage off Place House was often occupied with vessels bringing in coal from South Wales, and carrying back the copper ore from the mines up Carnon River. The little quay at St. Mawes had become a landing place for goods for the farms and hamlets of the Roseland. At regular intervals one of the fast smacks or cutters that linked London with Cornwall would be seen off the wall putting ashore packages or passengers from the great metropolis.

As a captain on half pay, reinforced by substantial sums of prize money, Richard might have settled easily into the quiet life of a country squire. He could have taken up his old activities of sailing, fishing and shooting. He might have joined the other local gentlemen in otter hunting up Percuil river, or coursing for hares, or playing bowls on the green at Gerrans. There were quieter pleasures too, such as visiting his many relations widely scattered about Cornwall, perhaps with one of his sisters riding pillion behind him.

But hunting, or taking tea in the afternoon, or candlelit evenings playing at cards were unlikely to appeal to a man accustomed to the bustle of life aboard a well ordered ship, and the excitement and variety of seafaring. He was soon approaching old friends to see if they could use their influence to get him a ship; Boscawen of course, and Sir Peter Warren, and Lord Anson, now at the Admiralty.

Even the interest of such important figures could not help him to a ship when none was available. Peter Warren, now M.P. for Westminster was a sick man[1]. Anson was deeply involved with naval reform and in particular trying to put an end to corruption in the dockyards. Besides there were several other captains, senior to Richard, and better known in the Admiralty who were importuning for the few ships that were available. Most of the bigger vessels were laid up "in ordinary", and there was little building of new ones. Like many another naval officer in peace time, he had to wait in patience. Not until October 1753, after more than three years on shore, did he receive the longed-for orders. Anson had been made First Lord of the Admiralty, and in spite of Government cheeseparing was getting small vessels into commission. Richard was to take command of H.M.S. "Garland", then lying at Plymouth.

The "Garland" was a frigate, a sixth rate carrying twenty-four guns mounted on one deck. She was a small vessel, only about 120 feet along the gun deck, and mustered a crew of 160 men. She had been first commissioned in 1748, and had spent the years since in the Mediterranean. At one time Richard might have regarded command of such a vessel as a step down in the world, for she had little more than half the tonnage of H.M.S. "Chester". But in a time of peace, there is no doubt that he counted himself fortunate as he hurried to Plymouth to take over the new ship.

The term "frigate" had been in use in the British Navy for over a hundred years. It described a small fast vessel that would not be expected to fight in the line of battle, but could be used as a ship of all work. In a fleet action she would carry messages, repeat signals, and assist damaged vessels. At other times she was used to protect convoys,

[1] He died in 1752, while on a visit to Ireland.

and guard the lines of communication against attacks from privateers or pirates. In the later wars against Revolutionary France, and the United States of America, big frigates with twice the hitting power of the "Garland" would provide some of the most stirring actions fought at sea.

But this was fifty years before that era, and England was nominally at peace with France. Richard's first orders in H.M.S. "Garland" were to take her in search of smugglers, for "free trading", which had been common enough among seafarers in every generation, had reached vast dimensions in the middle of the eighteenth century. It had passed beyond being the haphazard ventures of fishermen and coasting seamen, running in an occasional cargo on a dark night. By now smuggling had become a complicated business often well organised by wealthy merchants. It required not only fast and well manned vessels to run the contraband in, but a large number of ponies and escorts to carry it away to markets.

Although the outlay was considerable, so too were the profits. As an example, tea bought on the continent for seven pence a pound, could be sold in England for up to five shillings a pound[1]. Smuggled spirit might cost three shillings and sixpence a gallon ashore, while duty paid it cost eight shillings. Since an average sized vessel could land in a single run about 1500 ankers of spirit (each about 9½ gallons), as well as some twenty tons of tea, there were fortunes to be made by the principals, and even the humble tub carrier could make as much in one night as in a week of toil.

Almost everything was dutiable, and so almost everything was worth smuggling. Tin and woollens were carried outwards to the Continent, often hidden below honest cargo, while inwards came silk and tea, tobacco and brandy, playing cards, gin, sugar and chocolate. Although the running of such contraband was common to all coasts, it had become particularly rife on the southern shores of Devon and Cornwall. There were good logical reasons for this. Here were hundreds of sheltered landing places, in the open bays or in the creeks of such rivers as the Fal and the Tamar. In every port there were skilled sailors with seaworthy boats, men able and willing to risk a Channel crossing even on a winter's night. There was an abundance of small farmers equally ready to bring their horses to assist in a landing. Above all there

---

[1] In the 1750's of about four million pounds of the tea that was consumed annually, only about one fifth was believed to have paid duty.

was a ready market for tea and spirits, not only among the wealthy gentry, but among the poor tinners and fishermen.

Richard Spry was well aware of the extent of the trade along his own stretch of coast. He knew that several of the fishermen of St. Mawes and St. Anthony and Gerrans parishes took part. It was common knowledge that homeward bound East Indiamen would occasionally call into Falmouth where their decks became a sort of bazaar frequented by local country people in search of bargains. With rare exceptions the Customs men failed to act against the most flagrant examples of such tax avoidance. For it was also well known that it was almost impossible to get a conviction against smugglers in Cornwall.

Unlike many local gentlemen, Richard had little sympathy with the free trade[1]. He realised that the cost to the Treasury ran into hundreds of thousands of pounds, much of this going to the French in golden guineas. Moreover, he knew that if the Government failed to collect money in one form, it would need to raise it in others, such as increased Land taxes. Besides, he was well aware that if money did not come in there would be no new ships built, and no pay for sailors.

Thus when his orders came to cruise the channel to intercept smuggling vessels, Richard embarked on the execution of them with vigour. His base was Plymouth, but his area of operations was a triangle formed by the western end of the Isle of Wight, across to the Channel Islands, and westward to the Lizard. Every little harbour in those regions might be expected to shelter at least one experienced smuggler, but Guernsey in the islands, and Cawsand at the entrance of Plymouth Sound were recognised as the headquarters of the boldest of them.

Richard's orders required him to stop and search any vessel that he suspected of carrying illegal trade, but to be particularly vigilant in looking for wool and brandy. If any were found, the ship was to be taken to the nearest harbour and handed over to the Customs Officer. There was, however, an interesting footnote which said,

> "When you are on the other side of the Channel you
> are to endeavour to gain intelligence on what is doing
> in the French ports, and send us information thereof."

This last requirement was an indication that the uneasy peace

---

[1] Attitudes among the gentry were ambivalent. Sir Philip Hawkins, squire of Probus and M.P. for Grampound, dabbled in contraband, but left £600 to the Crown in his will, this being conscience money for unpaid duty.

signed at Aix la Chapelle five years before had already worn thin. There had been expressions of cordiality between Britain, France and Spain at that time, but nothing much had been settled. Moreover fighting had continued overseas. In India, each side sought the support of local rulers in their struggle for supremacy. In 1751, Robert Clive had captured, and then defended Arcot against the French-supported Nabob. In North America, the French from Canada had continued to push down the valleys of Ohio and Mississippi, and were building a line of forts from Montreal to New Orleans that would eventually block any westward expansion of the British settlers from their coastal colonies. There was no likelihood of peace there between the English colonists, and the French and their Indian allies. So in Europe both sides watched each other suspiciously, and began their warlike preparations.

The "Garland" made one short cruise, but any hopes Richard had of spending the winter pursuing smugglers into familiar harbours, were soon dispelled. In December he was given fresh orders that sent him with despatches to Carrickfergus in Northern Ireland, where he was to join Captain Gardiner of H.M.S. "Amazon". It proved a short but exciting voyage. The "Garland" arrived at night at the entrance of Belfast Lough in the teeth of a westerly gale that all but destroyed her. With no more than a dim beacon fire on Copeland Island to guide him, Richard had to drive the vessel hard to windward for only by carrying enough sail could she make any progress. They lost their jibboom, and their main topsail blew out. The main yard was sprung, and they were afraid that the foremast would go at any moment. It seemed they might be forced to run off before the wind, a hazardous course in such confined waters with the Scottish coast only a few miles to leeward. Eventually, tack for tack they reached a place where they could safely anchor, and there they rode out the gale, until Captain Gardiner could send a pilot to bring them under Carrickfergus Castle.

Captain Arthur Gardiner was most welcoming, for his was a lonely post in an exposed and uncomfortable anchorage. Yet it was a strategically important one, for from here ships could keep an eye on what was happening in Scotland. Gardiner was a bold and attractive character, soon to be promoted as flag captain to Admiral Byng aboard H.M.S. "Ramillies". He was in command of that ship when she fought in the abortive action off Minorca at the beginning of the Seven Years War. That was to be a humiliating experience, but years later he won a revenge of sorts by helping to capture the "Foudroyant" which had been the French flagship in that battle[1].

The "Garland" lay off Carrickfergus until the end of January when fresh instructions arrived, telling Richard to take his vessel to Cork on a recruiting cruise. His report to the Admiralty written from Kinsale several days later gives an interesting picture of the hazards faced by a sailing vessel on a winter passage.

As soon as he received his orders Richard embarked a coasting pilot. But the wind was blowing hard from the south-west and would not allow them to lay a course down the Irish sea. When as expected, the wind veered to the north-west, it blew so fierce a gale that they were unable to recover their anchors. Thus it was three days more before they got away with a favouring breeze. This carried them south and around the land until they reckoned they were off the entrance of Cork Harbour. But by now the wind had shifted to the south-east, and with it came such thick weather that the pilot was unwilling to close the shore. They were in that most dangerous of situations for a sailing vessel, uncertain of their position and close to a lee-shore.

At last the mist cleared a little and they could make out the land to starboard. The pilot declared that they were off the entrance of Cork, but when they stood in, it proved to be Oysterhaven, a lonely bay some six miles to the westward. They got out again with difficulty, and since by this time they were to leeward of their objective, Richard decided to make for Kinsale. As he explained in his letter,

> "I though it my best way as night was coming and an
> appearance of dirty weather, to push in for Kinsale,
> and secure that harbour, from whence I can make sure
> of a passage to Cork in a few hours, whenever the wind
> will permit."

That simple statement gives little indication of the anxious time he had just come through. In the event the weather did not ease for another six days, and by the time the "Garland" reached Cork, she had taken nearly two weeks to make a passage of about three hundred miles.

The south coast of Ireland had long been regarded as a fertile ground for naval recruitment, and among Richard's instructions was one which told him to take into the navy "all such lusty seafaring men as shall offer themselves". He was to bring his own ship's complement up

---

[1] Gardiner was killed in the action but he played a large part in forcing the 80 gun "Foudroyant" to surrender to H.M.S. "Monmouth" (60 guns).

to the maximum of 160 men, and should thereafter try to recruit a hundred more for other ships at Plymouth. But try as he might he could only find sixteen seamen to volunteer, although there was a great number of "Stout likely Young Fellows of Landsmen that offer themselves." Many of these would be simple country lads, some of them unable to speak English, and although they would have been welcome enough during war, in peace time they were not wanted.

Reports were now received of trouble in Bantry Bay where the Customs Officer at Berehaven had been murdered by Murtagh O'Sullivan, a notorious outlaw and smuggler. Richard was then back in Kinsale, and determined to set off in pursuit of O'Sullivan. But he was prevented from doing so by the onset of yet another fierce westerly gale. This wrought destruction even in the shelter of Kinsale, where there was a squadron of naval vessels under Rear Admiral Charles Watson waiting to sail for the East Indies. In the crowded moorings ships were soon in trouble. During one violent squall H.M.S. "Eagle" parted her cable and fell foul of H.M.S. "Bristol". Both vessels were only saved from driving ashore by cutting away their masts, but they were so damaged that Watson decided they must stay behind. Since the facilities for repairs were limited in Kinsale it was obvious that they must return under jury rig to the dockyard at Plymouth. Accordingly in mid April "Garland" was given the task of shepherding these two lame ducks back to England.

Richard's senior officer on this occasion was Captain George Pocock aboard H.M.S. "Bristol". Pocock was a robust seaman who had already made a name for himself in the West Indies. In 1747, after Hawke's victory in the second battle of Finnisterre, Pocock had intercepted a large part of the convoy which had escaped from Hawke and was making for the French islands. He was soon to be appointed rear admiral and sent with a squadron to India where he supported Clive, and helped to recapture Calcutta. At the end of the Seven Year War in 1763 he would further increase both his fame and his fortune, by taking a leading part in the capture of Havana.

Richard brought his important charges safely back to Plymouth and was sent once more on the anti-smuggling patrol. He was given particular instructions to look out for three fast luggers that had loaded in Guernsey, and were expected to slip across Cornwall in the first favourable wind. On this occasion he was almost successful. He intercepted two of the smugglers, but found that they had already been captured by Custom's cutters and had prize crews aboard. He went in pursuit of the third, but lost her in thick weather, only to find later she had landed her cargo in Gerrans Bay, to the eastward of Falmouth.

It was particularly provoking to Richard for this to happen on his home territory. Nevertheless, he had hopes for future operations. As he wrote to John Cleveland, Secretary to the Admiralty,

> "I am credibly informed by Gentlemen in the Neighbourhood that there are upwards of fifty sloops and boats go yearly to France from the adjoining Parishes of Veryan, Gerance and St. Anthony, ..... and as I am well acquainted with all the Gentlemen thereabouts they have assured me they will give me the most early Intelligence, if their Lordships would be pleased to continue me in that Station."

But their Lordships had other plans for his future. Their reply was to put him in command of another frigate, H.M.S. "Gibraltar", then fitting out at Portsmouth. The "Gibraltar" was a 6th rate, even smaller than the "Garland", and armed with only 20 carriage guns on a single deck.

Nevertheless she was absolutely new, having just been completed at Perrin Lock. She was an interesting vessel, being an exact copy of a privateer captured from the French which had been renamed H.M.S. "Tyger". Although her ship's company numbered only 140 hands, Richard found himself once more in the position of scraping around for trained seamen. He was allowed to take twenty from the "Garland", the rest he had to raise by the old methods of persuasion and pressing. The Admiralty refused him any from the guardships, saying "we expect you should procure men yourself." In the end he managed to get most of them, although he complained at one time that he had not more than five real seamen before the mast.

Among other matters, Richard was required to give a close report on the sailing qualities of the new ship. The original "Tyger" had earned a name for herself as an outstanding sailer, and their Lordships, ever mindful of the fact that the French were better naval architects than the English, were anxious to know how well the "Gibraltar" performed. It was a task that any seaman with a devotion to ships would delight in. His long report to Admiral Anson described how well she sailed; how after trimming her by shifting around ballast and stores so that she lay "3 foot two inches down by the stern, viz. afore 12ft.3 inches, abaft 15ft.5 inches", he had thereafter gone out of the Needles Channel and raced against two other frigates, H.M.S. "Speedwell" and H.M.S. "Savage", and left them standing on all points of sailing.

Her maiden voyage was from Portsmouth to Plymouth, taking Lord Edgcumbe and his retinue as passengers. Richard described their entry into Plymouth Sound thus,

> "It blew a fresh Gale, Smooth Water, and then we went nine knots, Close by the Wind, with a double reefed Fore and Mizen Topsail, Single reefed Main Tops'l, Jibb and Main topmast Staysail, and fore Course. She then lay along pretty much, the water coming in upwards of a strake in her Deck, and the Muzzles of our Guns in the Water."

For Richard Spry this description almost amounts to breaking into poetry, and certainly the "Gibraltar" must have made a brave sight on that day with her reefed sails bellying out and her lee rail down. His general summing up was that she was a fine fast vessel, although somewhat over masted, and therefore a little tender.

Perhaps it was Richard's enthusiastic account of "Gibraltar's" sailing ability that decided the Board of Admiralty to send her later on a mission of some importance, and one that was to cause him much anxiety. In November 1754 he was ordered to get his ship ready for a foreign voyage, and to await the arrival of Sir John Sinclair and some army officers. As soon as they were aboard he was to sail for Hampton Roads in Virginia, there to collect despatches from General Dinwiddie the Governor of the province, and return with them as quickly as possible.

The background to the voyage shows something of its importance. There had been serious news from North America, where the struggle had reached a new intensity. In northern Acadia there were constant skirmishes along the ill-defined border between the St. Lawrence and the Bay of Fundy, and the Canadians had recently built a strong fort there at Beauséjour. Their agents were busy again in Nova Scotia encouraging a spirit of revolt among the French Acadians. In the neighbourhood of Chebucto Bay where the British had built their new harbour called Halifax, the Indians were encouraged by the French to attack the settlers, being rewarded by gifts of blankets and guns. For their part, the British were offering handsome bounties to their own scalp hunters for bringing in Indian scalps[1].

From the other troubled scene, the valley of the Ohio where the Marquis Dusquesne had been strengthening French positions, the news was also bad. English traders were being taken prisoner, or driven away. Here too outlying farms and villages were targets for marauding Indians, who killed cattle, destroyed crops, and burned the houses, hatchetting and scalping the settlers. When Governor Dinwiddie sent troops to built a fort on the headwaters of the Ohio river, the French had taken possession of it and named it Fort Dusquesne.

Towards the end of 1754, the King's chief minister, the Duke of Newcastle, although wishing to avoid an extension of the conflict into Europe, yet felt that a show of force must be made in support of the American colonists. Accordingly a small squadron was made ready under Commodore Augustus Keppel, to carry two regiments of troops led by General Braddock. Now, carrying despatches, and to gain further information from Virginia, the Admiralty had decided to send H.M.S. "Gibraltar".

It was the kind of service on which the speed and weatherliness of a frigate would prove most important, and there is no doubt that Richard was anxious to show what he could do. But things went wrong from the beginning. When his orders came on the sixth of November, with the wind north-west and his vessel at anchor off Spithead, all seemed fair to proceed. But by the time his passengers were aboard, the wind had backed and was blowing a gale from the south-west. They were still there on the tenth, with Richard writing to the Secretary of the Admiralty,

> "About two in the Afternoon it blew hard with Rain and thick Weather, and looked very unsettled which determined me not to move till morning, at 6 it blew excessive strong which obliged us to strike yards and topmasts, and then it shifted to the S.S.W., and continues now about W.S.W. with thick blowing dirty weather."

He was caught in the classic dilemma that has troubled ships' masters since men first ventured to sea. Their orders and inclinations are to sail as soon as possible, but the situation and the weather are such,

---

[1] £150 was offered for the scalp of every Indian man over 16 years and half as much for the scalp of a woman or child.

that prudence demands that they should stay where they are. We can imagine Richard restlessly pacing his quarterdeck, eyeing the windvanes, staring to windward for the first signs of a shift in the weather. His anxiety was heightened by express letters from the Secretary, brought by messengers galloping through the night, demanding to know the reasons for delay. Their Lordships, showing unwonted anxiety, had been informed by Commissioner Hughes, the head of the dockyard, that the wind had been north-east by north the day before. This suggestions brought a spirited reply from Richard; "I must take leave to assure you that the Wind was never one hour to the Northward of East; as will appear I daresay by the Log books of every Ship at Spithead."

By the fourteenth of November he was under way, sending his last letter with the pilot as they sailed through the Needles Channel with a fine fair breeze. "I have great hopes of it (i.e. the east wind) coming on with the New Moon, and that I shall have no more occasion to make use of an anchor till I get within the Capes of Virginia."

Whatever Richard's delight at getting away at last, the ancient seafaring superstition of the moon affecting the weather did not prove well founded. The wind was soon back in the old westerly quarter. A fast frigate might have hoped, with reasonable conditions, to have done the voyage in thirty days. In fact they had a long and bitter passage of eight weeks, beating into violent gales between south-west and north-west, often with no more sail than a double-reefed mainsail.

Richard claimed that it was the worst weather that he had ever met with at sea. At one time the "Gibraltar" was almost overpowered, being struck by a squall that threw her on to her beam ends, "so that she lay for some time motionless with five strakes of her quarter deck below water." Only the fact that the sails she was carrying split to ribbons and so allowed the ship to come upright, enabled them to run her off before the wind. Nevertheless, Richard was full of praise for the "Gibraltar's" performance, saying it was more than many ships would have done in her situation.

He arrived at Chesapeake Bay on the eighth of January, 1755 and placed himself under Governor Dinwiddie's orders. In spite of the urgency of the Admiralty's demand for his return however, the ship was kept lying in Hampton Roads for weeks. Richard repeatedly pressed the Governor for permission to proceed, but he was kept back to await despatches from General Braddock.

While he lay there he was able to assess the situation in the colony, for he had several meetings with the Governor. Robert Dinwiddie was a Scot, and a very able man, but he had a difficult situation on his hands. Although the colonists of Virginia, Maryland and Pennsylvania were being hard pressed by the French on their northern borders, they seemed unable to submerge their own rivalries and jealousies. The result was confusion and lost opportunities.

Richard made several interesting observations in letters to John Cleveland. Mr. George Washington had been defeated, and made a prisoner in an attempt to recapture Fort Dusquesne. The French were reported to have an army of 11,000 men in Canada, and in the forts of the Ohio, although Richard observes, "I imagine the fears of the Virginians have greatly Augmented the Number of their Enemies."

Although he was not able to grasp the situation clearly he was witnessing the first definite moves in what was to become one of the most important wars in British history.

At last at the end of the month Richard was allowed to go, and made a fast passage, cracking on sail in the strong westerlies. He was back in Portsmouth in fifteen days, and went hurrying with the despatches personally to Whitehall. Clearly he had satisfied his masters, for within a few days he was promoted to the command of a Third Rate, H.M.S. "Fougueux", one of Vice Admiral Sir Edward Hawke's squadron, then lying in Portsmouth.

He handed H.M.S. "Gibraltar" over to a young Captain Holwall, and she became part of the same squadron. In the months that followed Richard would have plenty of opportunity to admire her grace and speed and weatherliness. She would earn further favourable notice some four years later serving in the Mediterranean under Admiral Boscawen. On that occasion "Gibraltar" was the frigate which detected the French fleet escaping out of the Straits, and her speed to windward enabled her to warn the Admiral, and so ensured the successful battle at Lagos[1].

[1] See page 150.

# CHAPTER IX

## THE WAR IN THE WEST

The seaport towns on both sides of the English Channel were full of rumours of war in that Spring of 1755. Although neither France nor Britain wished to begin the conflict, each was pressing on in a manner that would make it inevitable. The Admiralty, under Anson, was strengthening the Navy with faster and more heavily armed frigates. Guardships which had rotted uselessly at moorings for years were being fitted with guns, and completing their crews. The peacetime establishment of about eight thousand men was being rapidly increased by more than half as many again, using the usual methods of press and persuasion, reinforced by an increase in the King's bounty. The French were active likewise; English spies reported the gathering of squadrons of battle ships and frigates, and transports with more than three thousand troops assembled in the western ports of Brest and Rochefort.

The chief reason for all this preparation lay in America where the undeclared war had now intensified. The French again strengthened their claims on disputed territories in the Ohio and Nova Scotia. In reply British forces led by General Braddock were marching through the forests of Virginia to recapture Fort Dusquesne. Governor Shirley was about to move to Oswego on Lake Ontario, whence he would advance against the French positions at Niagara and Lake Erie, while yet another British column was to proceed to Lake Champlain against the fort at Crown Point.

The government, under the Duke of Newcastle decided on a further pre-emptive move. A strong fleet under Vice-Admiral Boscawen was to be sent to cruise off the entrance of the St. Lawrence with orders to seize any French ships attempting to land troops in Quebec or in Nova Scotia. As a member of this fleet Richard Spry's instructions were to take aboard the "Fougueux" six months supplies of all species, and "not to suffer a moment to be lost."

H.M.S. "Fougueux" was a third rate which had been captured from the French, being one of the vessels taken by Hawke off Finisterre in 1947. She was of fine design, like most of the French ships, and known to be a good sailer. The Navy kept her old name, which signified impetuosity, as well as her figurehead of a young woman with arms outstretched.

"Fougueux" was more splendid than any other vessel Richard had sailed in. Standing under the great lanterns at the poop his eye could range forward for 160 feet, taking in the rows of black iron guns on her main deck, the pine masts thick as boles of trees, the boats on their booms, the hatches, the hammock nettings, the square wall of the forecastle bulkhead. She could fire a broadside of thirty guns from two decks, and had a crew of five hundred and twenty men, to serve those guns and sail the ship.

While they were in Plymouth all the vessels took aboard their companies of soldiers for the passage to America - the "Fougueux" carrying the officers and men of Colonel Yorke's regiment. At the end of April they were on their way to the westward, Boscawen wearing his flag aboard H.M.S. "Torbay" and with eleven ships of the line and three frigates under him. Their plan of campaign was to proceed to Halifax, Nova Scotia, where they would join Commodore Keppel, and land their troops for service with General Braddock. They would then take station off Louisbourg, where they would carry out their orders to prevent the passage of any French men-of-war.

A few days after Boscawen had sailed, the French fleet slipped out of Brest. They sailed at night, without lights, but their departure was observed by British cruisers who reported them to be a formidable array of nineteen ships of the line and six frigates. If Boscawen met these he was likely to be overwhelmed, so reinforcements were despatched at once under Rear Admiral Francis Holburne.

Boscawen made his landfall off the south-east corner of Newfoundland at the beginning of June. Here he spread his ships out to cruise between Newfoundland and Cape Breton Island, with orders to bring in to the squadron any French men-of-war they might meet, - "which if they refuse so doing you are to compell them".

The "Fougueux" took up her station to the south of Newfoundland, some twenty miles from Cape Race. Richard had under his immediate command H.M.S. "Dunkirk" of 60 guns, whose captain was the Honourable Richard Howe. They soon met with a "Dogger", a large fishing vessel from the Grand Banks, which reported having seen several large ships with troops aboard. Otherwise there was no sign of any of the French fleet. It was a bad summer for fogs, even in those waters which are notorious for them. They came and went with bewildering rapidity. There were times when it was impossible to see the ship's foremast from her quarterdeck, and a fleet might ghost by at less than a cable's distance. Meanwhile, a mile away a vessel could be sailing in brilliant sunshine.

Richard's companion, Captain Howe was the younger son of an aristocratic family, with a long tradition of military service. He had already established himself as an able and intrepid young officer, for although he was only thirty years old he had seen much action in many parts of the world. In 1740, as a midshipman of fourteen he had sailed aboard H.M.S. "Severn" on Anson's famous voyage. That was a severe enough introduction to a seafaring life, for the "Severn" had been so battered off Cape Horn that she had been forced to return to England. Young Howe continued at sea however, and in the previous war had fought at La Guayra in H.M.S. "Burford", under Sir Charles Knowles. He continued to prosper, and thanks largely to his aristocratic connections was able to pass for lieutenant after only four years in the service. It was as we have seen, a bending of the rules not uncommon in the 18th century navy. As commander of H.M. sloop "Baltimore" at the age of nineteen he nearly lost his life and his vessel in a daring action against two heavily armed French privateers, during Charles Edward Stuart's rebellion.

Richard Howe and Richard Spry had much in common, for they had both served under the same commanders, and knew many of the same ships. Howe was said to be so taciturn and shy that some regarded him as almost inarticulate, and Robert Walpole described him as being "as undaunted as a rock, and as silent"[1]. But to others he was a gentle and generous friend. His crews called him "Black Dick" on account of his saturnine appearance, but they loved him. To them he was kind and considerate, and far ahead of his time in matters of treatment. After a battle he would visit the wounded in the ships' hospital, taking them wine and fruit from his own store.

Soon Richard Howe was about to show the other side of his nature. On the fifth of June, still on foggy weather, and now in company with the rest of the fleet, they came in sight of three of the French vessels.

---

[1] In time Howe would become one of the most distinguished of British admirals. He gave notable service during the War of American Independence, and the French Revolutionary wars. His most famous victory was that of the "Glorious First of June in 1794". (He was an ancestor of the present Princess of Wales).

Howe was ordered to intercept the nearest, which was the "Alcide" of 64 guns. He laid his vessel alongside and requested her captain, Monsieur Hocquart, to accompany him to join Admiral Boscawen. Hocquart asked whether they were at peace or war. Thereupon Howe repeated the order, and then seeing that the decks of the "Alcide" were crowded with soldiers and women, is said to have taken off his hat and requested that they should be sent below before he opened fire. This being done, each captain civilly asked the other to fire first. The action at close range then lasted for about quarter of an hour, by which time the "Alcide" was hammered into submission. Howe is reported to have cried to his crew at this point; "My lads! They have behaved like men; treat them like men".

The "Alcide" had on board some 900 people, mostly soldiers, as well as the Governor of Louisbourg, and £30,000 in silver. She was a notable prize and was taken to join Boscawen's fleet. The encounter is an interesting one showing something of the naval attitudes of the time. There was a degree of civility between the old enemies, a desire to defeat, but not destroy each other. It should be said, however, that this description of the incident comes from English sources. The French were very bitter about the affair, complaining that the "Alcide" was attacked without warning, and that it proved to be one more example of English perfidy.

A little later H.M.S. "Fouguex" was closely involved in the capture of another French vessel, this time in the company of H.M.S. "Defiance". They took the 64 gun ship "Lys", an easy prize however for she was sailing "en flute", that is with most of her guns dismantled to make room for troops and stores. After a chase of two hours she hauled down her colours, and Richard sent his first lieutenant to take command of her.

No one who witnessed these brief encounters could have realised that they were the opening blows in one of the most important wars in Britain's history. The French could not disregard such warlike actions, for an attack on men of war was a very different matter to fighting in the colonies. As soon as the news reached France they recalled their ambassador from London. Whereupon the British Admiralty issued orders authorising attacks on French vessels in all parts of the world, and formal declarations of war were made in the following Spring.

Apart from capturing the "Alcide" and the "Lys", Boscawen's blockade was not very successful. The rest of the French fleet passed by hidden by the fog. Several of the men o' war and store ships succeeded in reaching Louisbourg, while the remainder entered the St. Lawrence by way of the Straits of Belle Isle, a daring manoeuvre which carried them safely up to Quebec.

Boscawen continued his patrol off the St. Lawrence hopefully for a while. He had now been joined by Francis Holburne, and had under him a considerable fleet of nineteen battle ships and fourteen frigates or sloops. Richard was sent into Halifax with three prizes, the "Alcide", "Lys" and a French brigantine. From there he wrote to the Admiral,

> "Governor Lawrence will inform you that they are
> starving at Louisbourg, and if you prevent provisions
> being thrown into the Place they must eat one
> Another, or give it up".

That was too optimistic a picture. The French had learned from their previous loss of Louisbourg in 1744. Since then they had strongly fortified the place, and having just received fresh supplies had no intention of giving it up. In any case Boscawen's fleet was suffering from scurvy and typhoid, and he did not feel strong enought to mount a direct attack. So he maintained a small blockading force off Cape Breton, and sent most of his ships into Halifax.

Halifax[1], Nova Scotia, had been developed as a port since 1749 after Louisbourg was handed back to the French. It had been built on the shores of Chebucto Bay, and was already a well established town. The Chief Surveyor of Nova Scotia claimed it to be one of the finest harbours in the world; ..... "easy of access, capacious enough to hold all the Navy of England". Apart from the fortifications, there were several hundred houses and log cabins around the waterfront, with some two and a half thousand inhabitants. When Richard sailed in at the end of June he observed that it was crowded with French Canadian coasting vessels which had been seized by the navy.

In spite of its excellent harbour, however, Halifax was a poor place to be that hot summer. The sickness aboard the ships increased. From the "Fougueux" alone, three or four men were buried each day. Richard noted that out of his crew of five hundred, half of them were ill, one hundred and seventy four being in sick quarters ashore, and seventy others on board. Naturally, the foremast hands suffered most, but among the officers off duty at one time, he lists one Lieutenant, the

[1] It was named in honour of Lord Halifax

Master, the Gunner, the Carpenter, the Purser, eight Midshipmen and two Surgeon's Mates, "all extremely ill"[2].

Richard was not well himself, for as he wrote to Admiral Holburne, then in command of the port,

> "I will endeavour to wait on you in the cool of the evening to beg your permission to be on shore for two or three days, as the noise on board greatly affects my head and I cannot bear the sun."

At the same time he was writing to Boscawen,

> "I have smoak'd the ship, wash'd her well with Vinegar, and filld her full of Green Bows of Firs, Birch and Other Wood, but it has no effect, for within three days we have had upwards of thirty men taken down with Fevers, and I assure you Sir I shall think it the happiest days I ever met with when I get from this place."

Such attempts at hygiene were defeated by the overcrowding, for the ship carried British troops and French prisoners as well as its own seamen and marines. Moreover the chief killer was the deadly diet of salted food, and the scurvy caused by lack of vitamin C. For more than two centuries men had realised that long voyages would produce the same symptons, first fatigue and depression, then pains in gums and joints, and finally inability to stand, followed by haemorrhage, and death.

The cure took a deal of finding, although before the middle of the eighteenth century, a Scottish surgeon named James Lind had already provided the answer. While serving aboard H.M.S. "Salisbury" in 1747 he had made a number of controlled experiments which showed that oranges and lemons would cure the disease, and that cider also produced a good effect. He showed that other treatments common at the time, such as dosing with vinegar and sea water, or giving elixir of vitriol made the patient worse. In spite of the fact that he published his findings, the Admiralty ignored them for another forty years. Individual officers such as Boscawen took note however, and two world

---

[2] At the end of the summer he sent back to the Commissioners of the Navy at Whitehall 92 "Dead Men's Tickets", these being chits required for those who had died in the five months since they sailed. This was a large proportion of his ship's company in what had so far been a peaceful operation.

voyagers, Wallis in 1766 and Cook in 1768 showed what could be accomplished by the provision of fresh fruit, vegetables and clean water. But such were the powers of predudice and inertia in high places, that not until the middle of the nineteenth century was an issue of lime juice officially adopted in British ships[1].

Halifax was not a good place for seamen, even for those in reasonable health. There were of course the usual beer shanties, gambling booths and brothels, but apart from such dubious entertainment there was nothing to prevent the men from getting into trouble. They got drunk and quarrelsome. They went absent without leave, though where they hoped to escape is open to speculation. The land behind Halifax was high and rocky, covered with moorland and nearly impenetrable forests. One can only conclude that those who went that way were truly desperate for a little freedom. Most of them were brought back within twenty four hours, and were therefore accused of "straggling". Since this was not named as "deserting" which involved longer absence, it did not call for hanging. Straggling was punished by a fine, ranging from ten to forty shillings, according to the amount of reward that was paid to those who arrested the straggler.

A typical case was that of Samuel Shendrum of H.M.S. "Fougueux" who had the misfortune to be picked up by several men. The order to Spry concerning him, one of many similar, ran thus,

> "You are hereby required and directed to charge on your ship's books against Samuel Shendrum, Seaman, forty shillings for Stragling, having paid that Sum to those of a party of Soldiers who apprehended him, Stragling."

Forty shillings was a lot of money to a seaman, amounting to more than a month's pay, but no doubt Samuel felt it was better than being hanged at a yard arm, or flogged around the fleet. Yet there were plenty who suffered those penalties that summer. Court martials were held regularly, the crime ranging from desertion, to incitement to mutiny, or to striking an officer. In the space of little more than a month twelve men were executed for those offences.

There were other troubles for Richard to report. Some of the

---

[1] Although Lind had shown that lemon juice was more effective, lime juice was cheaper, and was produce of our own colonies.

prize crew put aboard the "Lys" led by the first lieutenant of H.M.S. "Fougueux", had broken into the cabins and trunks of the French officers. It had, wrote Richard, "the great appearance of a General Plunder." When his crew's quarters, and the lieutenant's cabin were searched there turned up silver cups, spoons and forks, a gold lined snuff box, several hundred silver coins, and much wearing apparel. Richard was moved to pity and fury at the distress of the French officers, and at his request the first lieutenant was removed from duty, and put before a court martial, although no mention is made of the result.

Meanwhile bad news had been coming from the frontiers. General Braddock's army on the other side of the Allegheny Mountains had suffered a heavy defeat before Fort Duquesne. They had marched, with colours flying and bands playing, along the forest trails until they had almost reached their objective. At which point the French and Indians, who were much more experienced in this kind of warfare, had set up an ambush, and cut them to pieces. Braddock was among those killed.

In his campaign along the Lakes, General Shirley had also been checked in his attack at Fort Niagara. Only from Beauséjour at the northern end of the Bay of Fundy was there any success to report. There a combined force of soldiers under Colonel Monckton, and ships under Spry's old comrade Captain Rous, had succeeded in capturing the fort, and driving the French from the region of St. John's river.

Any hopes Richard had of getting away from Halifax ended in the middle of October when Admiral Boscawen was ready to return to England. Winter was no time for campaigning in those waters, where there would be ice and fog and savage gales to contend with. It was also clear that no more supplies could reach the French in Canada or Cape Breton until the following Spring. Before he sailed Boscawen appointed Richard as the temporary commander in chief of the few ships he would leave behind in Halifax, as well as those in ports along the North American seaboard.

This was promotion indeed for Richard. As senior captain he now had under his command a squadron of four big men of war, fifty-gun ships and above, as well as ten frigates and sloops[1]. Although he was not given the title he was in effect a commodore. Yet with the honour went formidable problems. The ships he would control were

[1] See Appendix II.

widely scattered, separated by hundreds of miles of land as well as sea. He would be responsible for the protection of trade routes, harbours, and even isolated log built fortresses. It was a task that would call for tact, forethought, and resolution.

It was fortunate that among the captains left with him there were some notable characters. There was that vigorous and hard headed mariner Jonathan Rous in command of H.M.S. "Success". Another, the Honourable Samuel Barrington, captain of the "Norwich", (50 guns) had already begun to make a reputation for courage and enterprise. Barrington was the son of an Irish peer who had entered the navy in 1740 at the age of eleven. Due to his aristocratic connections his progress was meteoric. He was able to pass for lieutenant at the age of sixteen, although his papers claimed that he was then aged above twenty. It was another case of the rules being twisted for the right people. The young Barrington was immediately given the command of a sloop, and a year later, at the age of eighteen was post captain of a fifth-rate H.M.S. "Bellona". In his case such rapid promotion seemed to have been justified however, for in his first cruise he took as a prize the "Duc de Chartres" a French East Indiaman of considerable size. In later years as a rear admiral he performed some valiant work in the West Indies, during the American War of Independence. Now at Halifax Richard found him an amiable colleague and an efficient captain.

In complete contrast was Marriott Arbuthnott, a rough and hardy seaman of the old school. He had fought his way up through the service without influence, and although generally described as a blustering, foul mouthed bully, by sheer force of character he had gained command of Spry's old frigate H.M.S. "Garland". He was the type of captain often described in the sea literature of the time, as a "tarpaulin", and though he could be difficult to control, was well enough suited to an independent command on a distant station[1].

Among the other frigate captains was one who in time would become the most famous of all that company. This was Samuel Hood, in command of H.M.S. "Jamaica". He was older than Richard and had been at sea since 1731, but he was only the son of a Somerset rector, and without much "interest" his progress had been slow. His present ship was his first real command as a post captain. He had shown himself to be a most keen professional sailor with a good sense of naval tactics, and

---

[1] He stayed on in the navy to a late age, and fought not very successfully as an admiral during the War of Independence.

was above all a zealous officer prepared to take any action for the good of the service. In the future he too would have a long and successful career in both the American and French Revolutionary Wars. At the Battle of the Saints in 1782 he was rear admiral under Rodney, and took the surrender of the French admiral, De Grasse. He was one of those who bridged the gap between the navy of Anson and the navy of Nelson, for he was still serving in 1795 as Commander-in-Chief in the Mediterranean. His combination of dash, competence, and devotion to duty, helped to make him a model for the naval officers of that later time.

On 20th October Boscawen sailed for home with his armada of warships and transports, leaving Richard with the preoccupation of running his small fleet. In addition to the ever present problems of obtaining victuals and supplies and men for his own ship he had now to consider those of other vessels as well.

Boscawen had left him with one difficulty that had to be dealt with immediately. A complaint had been lodged, apparently by the entire lower deck of the frigate "Success", against their captain. This stated that among other things Captain Rous had encouraged his officers to beat the crew, and his purser to defraud them of their provisions. It complained that he had discharged men from the ship in return for bribes. Among other arbitrary and unjust acts he had "Entered on the Ships books, Women, Dogs, Cats and Names of Persons never heard of", clearly with the intention of defrauding the government of their pay.

Richard was required to enquire into these allegations and report back to the Lords Commissioners of the Admiralty at the first opportunity. He must have found it a painful duty when he remembered how he and Rouse had fought together at Annapolis Royal. Some of the crimes complained about were not unknown among certain naval captains, but Rous was not such an officer. However, in due course the five captains of all the men of war in the harbour were ceremoniously rowed out to the "Success" to enquire into these "divers Acts of Arbitrariness and Injustice".

Having made enquiries first among the commissioned and warrant officers, and examined the Ship's Books without finding any evidence of malpractice, they mustered the rest of the ship's company. Richard wrote,

"When the complaint was read to them they seemed greatly surprised, and when we told them we were come to enquire into and redress their Grievances, they to a Man declared they never hear the least Syllable of it before, and that they never desired to sail with a better Captain or Officers as long as they lived, that they had never been ill treated by either, or had any part of their provisions stopped from them, and seemed greatly exasperated against the person who writ the Complaint".

Further enquiries revealed that the complainant, a seaman named David Sutherland, was no longer aboard the ship, but was in prison, where he had been sentenced to a spell in the pillory for fraud and forgery! So Captain Rous was vindicated. Nevertheless the incident is important, and has been quoted at length, for it shows that even in a period as heartless and corrupt as the eighteenth century, in a service as hard as the Navy, the authorities were concerned, on occasion at least, to see that justice was done.

Richard was soon involved in a far less creditable incident, which concerned the French Acadians, the old inhabitants of Nova Scotia. Sir Charles Knowles had suggested during the previous war after the threat to Annapolis that they should all be transported, and English settlers brought in their place, but the Government had taken no action. The Acadians, known to the British as "neutral French" were of course in an impossible situation. The British forced them to profess loyalty to King George while their fellow countrymen declared them to be rebels, and threatened them with execution if they refused to fight against him. Most of them were illiterate but hard-headed peasants. They loved Old France, although they would not supply New France (Canada) with goods unless paid for in cash. Equally they hated the English but would cheerfully work and trade with them in return for payment.

Although the Acadians had shown on many occasions that all that most of them wanted was to be left alone to fish, or tend their land, yet their presence was once more regarded as a threat, particularly to Annapolis and Halifax. With a new war imminent the British government now decided to move them out of Nova Scotia altogether. Orders came that they were to be rounded up and transported to other parts of the American colonies.

Much of this unpleasant duty fell to Richard Spry and his

captains. Naval and merchant ships were sent to the main ports of the
Bay of Fundy, and under the direction of their crews the Acadians were
driven from their homes. Most of the Acadians had been there for
generations, but they were forced to go with little notice leaving many of
their possessions behind. It meant the breaking up of communities, and
the parting of old friends, a bitter process later described by Longfellow
in his poem "Evangeline". However, few of the English seamen seemed
to have felt much sympathy for them. More typical was a comment by
Captain Matthew Dixon who wrote to Richard from Annapolis Royal,

> "The French Scoundrels are embarking and will be
> compleated in three or four days, when I shall give a
> Huzza, and two extra ordinary ones when they get out
> of the Gut. I heartily hope that we shall be able to have
> always the upper hand of these perfidious Villains,
> who would not hesitate to Murder us all to gain one
> single advantage."

Captain Dixon was particularly upset by the fact that some of
the Acadians had been escaping into the woods, and leaving behind
booby traps such as loaded muskets facing their farm doors. By early
December most of the unhappy Acadians were on their way to Boston.
Between four and five thousand were transported together, men,
women and children crammed aboard small vessels, to be taken
eventually to the Carolinas.

While Richard expressed no particular antipathy to the victims
of the policy he was carrying out, he was soon roused to considerable
fury when he discovered that the Governors of Georgia and South
Carolina, who had not welcomed the move, were proposing to send
some of them back. He sent orders to Captain Samuel Hood to stay in
southern waters, to intercept any vessels with returning Acadians and
put them back ashore in the Carolinas. In the end however those
particular refugees wisely decided to go on to the French territory of
Louisiana where they settled around New Orleans, and there became
the "Cajuns", preserving in the deep south the language, music and
traditions of Old France which they had brought from Nova Scotia.

Richard's attention was now taken up by a small campaign being
waged on the Great Lakes. From time to time he received despatches
from Captain Houseman Broadley, commander of the sloop "Oswego"
operating on Lake Ontario. These messages brought by canoe and

along forest trails to Boston, and thence to Halifax by schooner, took nearly two months to reach Richard. The perils of the journey were such that although duplicates and even triplicates of despatches were sent, not all of them got through.

Broadley with his own vessel, and a new one named the "Ontario" which they had just built on the lake had been engaged in supporting Governor Shirley's campaign against Fort Niagara. But Shirley who had done so well as a tactician in 1745 had failed to make any headway in the new struggle. The winter came and the expedition was brought to a halt. Spry was very critical of Shirley's proceedings, or perhaps the lack of them. Writing to Admiral Boscawen now back in England, he said,

> "Notwithstanding the great things we were taught to expect from Shirley's Wisdom and Johnson's Courage, neither of them have attempted the least thing since Dieskaws defeat ..... The People of Boston are not at all satisfied with these proceedings, and say they wou'd much sooner have met with a defeat than not have made an attempt."

Captain Broadley's letters to Richard, and his replies all tend to show aspects of the same old problem. The campaign was suffering from lack of money, and from lack of men. Broadley tells that the French are building five new vessels on the Lake, and the Congress of American Governors in New York had decided to build only two brigs and a sloop to match them. Moreover seamen for the ships were only contracted to serve in the summer, and most of them went back to the coast for the winter, and how to get them with the poor wages offered he did not know. Spry's reply was not particularly helpful. "Get them by any means possible", he says, but "you must act with the utmost frugality". Meanwhile he would be having bills printed in Boston offering an advance of 30/- sterling to seamen who would volunteer for service in any of His Majesty's ships. This was frugality indeed for it represented less than a week's pay for the average merchant sailor on those coasts. As might be expected it had little effect.

The anxiety and frustration caused by manning came out starkly in page after page. Writing in January 1756 to Captain Marriott Arbuthnot, Richard says,

> "I hope to God you will be Able to procure us some

Seamen, as 'twill be impossible for us to act like English Men of War without them. I have buried from my own Ship above 140, and upwards of a hundred more have died that were left Sick by Adml Boscawen's Squadron, Exclusive of what the rest of the Ships have lost, so that you may easily conceive the Situation we must be in if not assisted by the Stations Ships. I propose being at Sea by the first of May at furthest and shall be extreamly glad to see you before that time."

They were then half way through the winter, all the big ships laid up, sails unbent and running rigging unrove. Movement between Halifax and the outside world was greatly restricted, and the only contact with Boston, London or the rest of his squadron was by small sloops and schooners. Supplies of food and fuel ran low, and life was made difficult by freezing fog. Nevertheless it seems the weather in Nova Scotia that winter was kinder than usual, with few storms and not more than three days severe frost at a time. Richard notes that the gales there were not as frequent or severe as those he had experienced off the coast of Virginia, or Massachusetts. On calmer warmer days, they took the opportunity of careening their ships, hauling them down and scraping and burning off the summer's growth. At such times too ships' crews were employed in building a wharf and reservoir on George's Island in Halifax harbour with spouts that would convey water into four longboats at once. He records in a report to John Cleveland; "it won't cost the Government Twenty Pounds, whereas if it had been built by any Person here it would not have cost less than Three Hundred."

In the same report he notes that there is still a good deal of sickness, and the men only recover slowly, "tho' I have taken care to see that they want for nothing." He adds, with evident pride, that since the fleet had sailed back to England, not a man had tried to desert, although he omits to mention that there had still been several cases of straggling.

By the end of February the next campaign began to take shape. News came from Annapolis that the French were on the move from Canada preparing to recapture their old fort at the entrance of the St. Johns River, across the Bay of Fundy. There were also reports that one of the transports which had been carrying two hundred and seventy deported Acadians from Annapolis to Boston, had been seized by the Acadians and taken into St. Johns River. The same people, had also captured a New England schooner and having taken her stores had burned her. In that same troubled area, in the Bay of Passamaquoddy, French Indians had seized a schooner from Boston and were reported to be turning her into a commerce raider. These were small skirmishes but they could not be ignored. Richard wrote to Governor Shirley concerning the captured schooner,

> "She is a large Vessel, near Eighty tons, with 8 swivel
> guns, and may do great mischief in the Bay of Fundy if
> not totally destroyed or taken which I shall Instantly
> Endeavour to do."

The idea of Red Indians capturing a large sailing vessel and going on the warpath in her, is a novel one to us. Yet many of the coastal tribes produced good seamen, and there were frequent complaints from fishermen of being attacked by red skinned "pirates".

Indians were of course playing an important part in the struggle that was taking place in the wilder regions of lake and forest. From Lake Ontario, young John Laforey, captain of the sloop "Ontario" wrote that the French had asked the Indians of the Five Nations for permission to march through their territory to attack Oswego. This was the main British base in the lake, and was a strongly built stone fort with a good harbour. Fortunately the Iroquois hated the French and had refused permission. So Laforey was getting his ships ready to meet an attack by water. His final letter to Richard written in April showed that things were not going very well. The fort was surrounded by French Indians who were scalping and carrying off his people, and messages only got through with difficulty. Captain Broadley who had been expected for some time with a body of seamen and naval stores had not arrived. Laforey had forty carpenters at work preparing the new vessels but had been "a good deal impeded by the Weather and the Scalping Indians." All was in vain, for Oswego was captured by Montcalm later in the year, although Laforey was able to escape.

Richard was now using every opportunity to get his big ships ready for sea, intent on blockading Louisbourg and the St. Lawrence as soon as the weather allowed. They were desperately short of naval stores, particularly new rope for the running rigging, until the timely arrival of a store vessel from England solved that difficulty. But as ever, the great bogy was the lack of men. He wrote to General Shirley of Massachusetts, and the governors of the other colonies, begging their aid in raising volunteers, for every one of his men-of-war was over a hundred men short. He had many promises but few men in return.

In desperation Richard now put two of his sloops, the "Mermaid" under Captain Washington Shirley and the "Hornet" under Sampson Salt to patrol off Boston, with orders to press every man they could out of incoming English merchant vessels. As a result of these orders he had endless complications however, for Captain Salt in an excess of zeal pressed some fishermen, and four sailors out of an American coasting vessel. Protests flowed in from Governor Shirley, as well as many of the Boston merchants. There was such an uproar "that it had like to put a Stop to publick business." So Richard had to send fresh orders for the release of the pressed men, explaining to Shirley,

> "I am too great a friend to the Colonies to think of procuring a Single Man to the prejudice of any of them, particularly those of Massachusetts Bay where I have formerly received so many Civilities."

Unfortunately for Richard that was not the end of the matter for it continued to bring him trouble throughout the summer. It reached its peak when two of the "Hornet's" men were set upon by a mob while on shore in Boston, and dragged before the magistrates on the charge of illegal impressment. To Richard's indignation the British seamen were clapped in jail, and he had to write demanding their release. He took a very strong line over this, and in retaliation ordered his captains to seize two of the best men out of every colonial trader or fishing vessel they might meet with, until the "Hornet's" seamen were released. He was truly angry with the New Englanders for what he regarded as treachery to their mutual war effort. He complained not only about their attitude on the subject of pressing, but the fact that some of their merchants were smuggling stores to the enemy in Louisbourg.

Clearly the American colonists had raw nerves on the matter of press gangs, for Samuel Hood found similar problems in Charleston, South Carolina. He arrived there on passage to the Bahamas with his sails blown to ribbons. While he was making new ones he tried to press some seamen in the port. The result was as he explained to Richard, "I have some many writs out against me I dare not go ashore."

The sharp reaction of the American colonists, particularly those of Boston, against what the regarded as high handed behaviour by the

British navy forms an interesting portent of things to come. For much the same deep feelings, twenty years later, those same people would be involved in actions against authority that would lead to the War of Independence.

In the midst of all this bother messages were coming from the outlying settlements of Fort Cumberland and Fort Monckton, on the Chinecto peninsula, in the disputed territory north of the Bay of Fundy. Both of the forts were under pressure from the French, and both were short of stores particularly gun powder and match. Colonel Hill from Monckton told of losing ten men out of a party of thirty soldiers who were ambushed by Indians within a few hundred yards of the fort. Colonel Scott at Fort Cumberland wanted men to replace the New England troops who were due to return home. Scott was something of a fire eater. If only he could have a couple of hundred troops and a few whale boats, "he would haul them across the isthmus into the Bay Vert, and with two hundred Rangers and one or two of your Frigates would sweep the whole coast of French and Indians." The soldiers' pleas were supported by those of Charles Lawrence, Governor of Nova Scotia, who knew well enough that those two forts were his front line of defence. But Richard, short of men, material and ships, resolutely stuck by his main task of guarding the approaches to Cape Breton and St. Lawrence.

In spite of all his problems with Acadians, Indians and Bostonians, Richard managed to get his little fleet to sea in time, and was cruising off Louisbourg by the middle May. He was rewarded almost at once with success. Off the port they fell in with the "Arc-en-Ciel", a French 50 gun ship, full of troops, and also a store vessel loaded with guns and soldiers, both of which were captured without a struggle. But then came the usual vile weather, continual fog and gales of S.W. wind that made station keeping off Louisbourg almost impossible. Nevertheless he remained there for nine weeks, before returning with some of his vessels to Halifax. His return was due in part to the need for more men for he had been required to send many of them with the prizes he had taken.

At Halifax he found that Commodore Charles Holmes had arrived with H.M.S. "Grafton" and H.M.S. "Nottingham" a fortnight earlier, and had put to sea accompanied by two of the sloops to look for him. They had missed each other in the fog although Holmes ran into a larger force of four French vessels coming from Quebec. This led to a brisk action with ships damaged on either side, but neither was strong enough to force the issue. So the French went into Louisbourg, and Holmes returned to Halifax.

Commodore Holmes brought with him the news that war had been declared in the middle of May. Holmes was an energetic and efficient officer, only a few years senior to Richard. He now took over the command of the squadron, but undoubtedly recognised that the difficulties and hardships of the long winter deserved some reward. He therefore sent Richard on a cruise with "Fougueux" and the "Centurion" to explore as far as the Seven Isles in the Gulf of the St. Lawrence. He was required to,

> "Take, Sink, Burn or otherwise destroy all Ships of War or other Ships or Vessels belonging to the French King or his Subjects, and to Annoy and Distress them in the Best and Effectual Manner you are able."

Richard, and Captain Mantell of the "Centurion" set about their task with diligence. The western entrance of the Gulf of the St. Lawrence, from Cape Breton to Cape Rosier was an area strewn with bays and islands. Here there were scores of tiny settlements, where, as on the opposite shores of Newfoundland, the inhabitants were devoted to the catching and preserving of fish. Here on wooden jetties and specially built stages the cod caught along the shore was gutted and split, salted and dried in wind and sun, and stacked to be shipped later to Europe. Salt cod formed an important part of the diet of peasants in Southern countries, and was a valuable contribution to the economy of France. The waters between the settlements were busy with small craft, fishing boats and trading vessels, schooners and snows, shallops and sloops.

Into this busy scene swooped the "Fougueux" and "Centurion", with little to oppose them other than muskets in the hands of enraged fishermen. They burnt and destroyed as directed, taking some vessels and cargoes as prizes to be sent back to Halifax. Their most successful area of operations was in Gaspé Bay, on the south-east side of the entrance into the St. Lawrence River. Here they captured a couple of schooners, a large sloop commanded by an old man of ninety, and took several shallops full of dried fish and beaver skins which they kept, and one containing "two very fine girls", which they allowed to go. Then having burnt the port of Little Gaspé to the ground went their way with no more than a few men wounded from buckshot.

Richard was full of praise for the amenities of Gaspé Bay, commenting that as many as twenty-five large traders came every year from St. Malo to load fish there, and that it would shelter a squadron if needed. He took soundings and prepared a chart for future use. The two ships then sailed into the St. Lawrence intending to cruise as far as Seven Isles on the north side of the estuary, but were driven back by a series of hard gales from the North West. Finally they ran for Halifax, with their sails split and topsides damaged, reaching that port at the end of September.

It was Richard's last operation off the American coast for that year. A few weeks later Holmes sent him home with despatches for the Admiralty. The "Fougueux" made a good passage and arrived in Plymouth early in November. She was warped into Dock for repairs, and Richard after his journey to see their Lordships was given brief leave.

Life had taken another series of dramatic turns. His brother Arthur had died during the past winter, and all the broad acres of St. Anthony had become Richard's. Now he might have felt was the time to resign his commission and become the squire at Place. But he could not give up his old way of life, and no doubt felt it would be wrong to do so. He could afford to hire others to look after his property. In addition to his captain's pay and the large sums of prize money he had won, his duties as commander in chief at Halifax was rewarded with an extra ten shillings a day.

He left his sisters at Place, and returned to Plymouth. His decision to continue in the service had an immediate reward. This was the command of H.M.S. "Orford", a fine third rate, bigger than the "Fougueux", and of new construction.

# CHAPTER X

## H.M.S. "ORFORD" AT LOUISBOURG 1757/8

When Richard joined his new command in mid February, she was lying at anchor in Plymouth Sound ready for sea. He sailed at once taking under his charge a convoy of fifteen merchant vessels bound for Portsmouth. They had a pleasant passage for the time of year, and when he arrived at Spithead, Richard found he was to serve under the flag of Vice Admiral Sir Francis Holburne. A fleet was being collected for an attack once again on the fortress of Louisbourg.

The ships assembled at Spithead consisted of twelve of the line, and five smaller rates, with sufficient transports to carry seven regiments. More ships and men were to join them in southern Ireland. There were the usual delays in getting men and stores. Richard had been allowed to take forty of the crew from H.M.S. "Fougueux", but as he wrote to Mr. Jackson, the purser of that vessel, he wished he could have taken many more. Meantime he had trouble with one of his more important officers aboard "Orford". This was the master, who had been injured by a fall during the passage to Portsmouth, and had been put ashore in sick quarters at Gosport. When he failed to return Richard sent one of the lieutenants to find the reason, and discovered that he had gone missing several days before.

Vice-Admiral Holburne was a Scot whose wealthy connections had brought him to flag rank. He had been second in command to Boscawen in the operations off Cape Breton in the previous year, and although Anson thought well of him, Boscawen did not. Certainly on this occasion he seemed to lack the necessary drive for mustering a large fleet. Perhaps this was partly due to the fact that the naval authorities in Portsmouth were concentrating their attentions on the drama of Admiral John Byng.

It will be remembered that Byng had failed to relieve Port Mahon in the first year of the war, and so had lost the valuable Mediterranean base at Minorca. Now he was to pay the penalty, and

Richard Spry was one of the captains ordered to attend his execution aboard H.M.S. "Monarch" on Monday, March 14th. There were many who disagreed with the court martial's findings, but Richard made no comment, at least on paper. Voltaire said that in England they shot an admiral from time to time "pour encourager les autres", and there can be little doubt that it helped to sharpen the attitudes of many naval officers.

Holburne got his fleet away at last in the middle of April, and proceeded to Cork to collect the rest of his ships and troops. He now had fifteen large fighting ships and nine small, as well as a great number of transports. His second in command was Charles Holmes, Richard's senior officer of the previous year.

There were many other old friends among the fleet. One was Captain William Mantell, still in command of H.M.S. "Centurion". Another was Hugh Palliser, captain of the "Eagle". Richard first met Palliser in 1748 when he brought the frigate "Sheerness" to join Boscawen's fleet in India, and with it the welcome news that peace had been signed. He was said to be a difficult man to deal with, but deserves much credit for his recognition of the genius of James Cook. Palliser had been made captain of the "Eagle" soon after Cook joined her as an able seaman, and had recommended him for promotion as master's mate, - the first step on his way to becoming the outstanding navigator of his time[1].

The voyage across the Atlantic against strong westerly winds was a slow one, with the usual exciting problems of keeping the transports together. They did not arrive off the coast of Nova Scotia until the ninth of July, three months after leaving Portsmouth. Meanwhile the French, well aware of what was happening, had slipped two convoys into Cape Breton and the St. Lawrence.

In Halifax the British met with an additional force under Rear Admiral Sir Charles Hardy. He had come with a convoy from New York, loaded with militia and rangers from the colonies. There would be many older men among them who would remember the success they had in taking Louisbourg eleven years before. Together they formed a formidable fighting force confident of their ability to capture that fortress again.

The overall command of the American forces was in the hands of

---

[1] It was largely due to Palliser's recommendation that Cook was sent in command of the "Endeavour" to the South Seas.

Lord Loudoun, who had left the defence of the New England states to provincial troops, and planned to use his main forces first against Louisbourg, and then Quebec. While the ships were stored and watered after their long passage, the soldiers were landed and exercised. Then came some bad news. Scouting frigates reported that the French fleet in Louisbourg, under Admiral de la Motte was of almost equal strength of that of the British. It was followed by reports that a French-Canadian force under General Montcalm had advanced into New York state and captured Fort William Henry on Lake George. Lord Loudoun wisely decided that the risk of attacking Louisbourg was too great, and returned with his troops to New York to defend that state.

Admiral Holburne, left in Halifax, and perhaps with memories of what had happened to Admiral Byng, now decided to make a fighting gesture. He set out with his fleet of 26 sail[1] to trail his coat outside Louisbourg, and attempt to bring the French ships out to action. He arrived off the port, but the French made no move to accept the challenge.

Instead an older and more dangerous enemy now came into the action. On the twenty-fourth of September the blockading fleet was struck by a sudden and violent storm, one that could have altered the whole history of Nova Scotia, and perhaps of Canada. The evening had been fair and calm, so that several of the ships were on their station close to the harbour mouth. Out of the south east came a sudden strong wind, with mist and rain, a gale which by midnight had developed into a hurricane. Many of the British ships were trapped close to a lee shore, and they were soon engaged in a desperate struggle for survival. There had been barely time to lower their topgallant masts and reef sails before the blow struck. All that night and through the misty dawn they struggled to claw their way seawards, and it says much for the hardihood and skill of the crews that only one of the big ships was lost. That was the "Tilbury" of 60 guns which was driven on to the rocks, and some three hundred of her men drowned. A shift in the wind early on the following day saved the entire fleet from disaster. The wind veered, first south-west and then west, and although it continued to blow a gale, it was now off shore.

A note in the "Orford's" log says, "At noon wore ship to S.W.'d. Saw several of our ships some of them having lost masts. Saw the land N.W. to N., distance 4 or 5 miles, after the wind shifted to the

[1] See Appendix II.

Westward." It is a brief enough observation for such a severe struggle, but doubtless they had their hands full. All of the ships had suffered, although "Orford" less than most. Richard lists his damage in a report to Admiral Holburne.

> "The Tiller broke in the Rudder head, A Topsail Yard carried away, Pump Winches broke. Main Sail, Main Staysail, Jibb and Fore staysail entirely Blown away. Cutter broke lose and Stove in. One main shroud broke, Main Mast Sprung in the Lower Deck Partners, Rudder Head much Twisted and Split. Twenty Barrels of Powder damaged in the Magazine."

*H.M.S. Terrible of 74 guns (after a line engraving by R. Short in 1748). A Third Rate captured from the French in 1747 she was taken into the British Navy and served with Spry at Louisberg in 1757.*

He also records that he spoke with Captain Marshall of the "Nottingham", which had a shattered bowsprit and foremast, and her hands were rigging a jury mast for the main. The rest of the fleet was scattered far and wide, those which were able towing the dismasted ones some making for Newfoundland, some for Halifax, some for England. Among the latter was Commodore Charles Holmes in the "Grafton" who had lost his rudder, and bore away for home with a jury rudder made from a spare topmast.

The French fleet, even in the shelter of such a fine harbour as Louisbourg had suffered also. Ships dragged their anchors and got foul of each other. A frigate was driven ashore, and some twenty five merchantmen and twice as many fishing vessels wrecked. We have a graphic account from a French observer who wrote,

> "Sailors who have been more than fifty years afloat say they never saw the sea so awful. The ramparts were thrown down and water inundated half the town."

He adds that the French looked out next day expecting to see the coast covered with wrecks, for they imagined that it would be impossible for the British fleet to win clear of the land. But what they saw was,

> "All their ships were scattered and dispersed, five of them were seen together, driving before the wind towards Newfoundland without masts, ..... In short it was evident that five French men of war if they had gone out of the harbour in quest of the English, would have been sufficient to pick up all that was left of the English fleet."

But Admiral de la Motte failed to take that step and so missed the chance of a resounding victory. Instead Admiral Holburne was allowed to gather together those ships that were able to do their own repairs, among them the "Orford", until he had under him a squadron of seven valiant ships. One does not need to underline the difference in attitude between the two commanders. No doubt De la Motte had his problems with gale damage and sickness among his crews. But it is astonishing that he remained in port with his powerful fleet while Holburne was able to return unmolested to Halifax, with at least one small fighting force.

Clearly there would be no more campaigning in that year. There were not the facilities for repairing so many damaged vessels in Halifax, and in mid-November Admiral Holburne took most of them back to England. He left nine which were in reasonable order behind, including H.M.S. "Orford", with Lord Alexander Colville as their commander in chief.

Admiral de la Motte later slipped out of Louisbourg and across the Atlantic, avoiding the blockade off the west coast of France and safely entering Brest harbour. For this success he was rewarded with a pension of twelve thousand livres! He hardly deserved that, for not only had he been quite ineffectual, but he had brought back with him so much scurvy and fever that the entire port of Brest was brought to a standstill for the rest of that winter. It is hardly necessary to stress the difference in treatment of La Motte and Byng.

For the British squadron left behind it meant another long spell of darkness and cold. The ships were kept in readiness for sea, but most of their time was spent at anchor. Whenever the weather permitted a group of seamen was landed from the ships to spend the day building a careening wharf on George Island. It was a popular service for they received an extra 6d a day's pay, and "an Allowance of Grogg (half a pint) over and above their Spruce Beer every day they were sent." The rest of the time in the short winter days was spent on the eternal maintenance, routine repairs of sails, spars and rigging, and watering and storing ship.

Although the bigger men o' war kept in harbour, merchant vessels were shuttling to and fro between Halifax and the American ports, and had to be protected. H.M.S. "Orford" was put in charge of a small armed schooner, the "Monckton" which under First Lieutenant Cosby was kept cruising off the coasts of Nova Scotia. Among her more successful ventured was the re-capture of the "Endeavour", a sloop from Boston which had been recently taken by a Louisbourg privateer. Lieutenant Cosby brought her back into Halifax as a prize, with the French crew as prisoners.

The long winter gave Richard the opportunity to get to know his other colleagues better. One who particulary impressed him was Edward Hughes in command of the "Somerset". Hughes was a first class seaman, and a man of noted courage. Many years later, as a rear admiral, his skill and obstinacy in a series of actions against the French in the East Indies helped to preserve India for British rule. But he never earned a great name outside the service. He was too much of a traditionalist, and his fear of breaking the established rules of war, prevented him from achieving great victories.

In the middle of March 1758, H.M.S. "Captain" arrived from England, bringing Rear Admiral Sir Charles Hardy to take over the squadron. Within three weeks they were at sea, blockading Louisbourg and the St. Lawrence once more. They had a hard time of it, for the weather was vile, the sea was covered with fields of floating ice, and on several occasions the ships were trapped among the floes. Because of the weather they were unable to maintain close blockade and prevent reinforcements from entering Louisbourg. The French had managed to slip several small squadrons out through the blockade at Brest, and these made remarkably good passages across the Atlantic.

Eventually the main body of the British force under Boscawen arrived, having suffered a frustrating voyage of calms and head winds. They had taken the traditional route to the south by way of the north east trades, but had failed to find favourable winds and had been eleven weeks on passage[1].

Boscawen's fleet represented a determined attempt to finally settle the problem of the American colonies. The failures of the first years of the war, and particularly the loss of Minorca, had brought William Pitt into power as Secretary of State. Pitt was the ablest strategist of his time, and he recognised that Britain's main effort must be to make full use of its naval power and mercantile strength. The French armies had proved more than her equal in Europe, but there Pitt would bolster Frederick the Great of Prussia with supplies and subsidies. Meanwhile British ships would blockade the coasts of France, destroy their trade, strike sudden blows on their coasts, and above all expel them from North America. He declared that the war had been undertaken, "for the long-injured, long-neglected, long-forgotten people of America". This was only partly true, but it was a policy that would have the full support of the colonists as well as of Anson at the Admiralty, and Boscawen and Hawke at sea.

Pitt had decided on a fresh full scale attack on Canada, and he was determined there would be no failure this time. The troops were in the charge of General Amherst, a most able and painstaking soldier, who had under him the brilliant young Lieutenant General Wolfe. The plan included a force to be sent under General Abercrombie, which

---

[1] A French squadron which left Brest a month after Boscawen had sailed from England, reached Louisbourg two weeks before he arrived at Halifax.

would move by way of Lake George and Champlain towards Montreal. Another army led by Brigadier Forbes would go through Pennsylvania against Fort Dusquesne. But the most important blow would be by Boscawen against Louisbourg, still the key to the St. Lawrence, Quebec, and Canada.

Boscawen had come out in the newly built H.M.S. "Namur", the second ship to carry that name, -with Matthew Buckle as flag captain. After their initial delay they set about operations with their usual enthusiasm, and by mid-May had sealed all the approaches to the Gulf of St. Lawrence. Meanwhile in Halifax the army had been preparing with equal resolution. Carpenters had pre-fabricated gun platforms, and carts for transporting the artillery across marshy ground. Wolfe had been exercising his troops in regular manoeuvres, rehearsing landings from transports, and skirmishing in the thick woods. Many of his troops were those who had come out the year before, and who had spent the winter in America. Wolfe, never easily satisfied, remarked that their spirit was all right, "but the army is undone and ruin'd by the constant use of salt meat and rum." It was a comment that any naval captain would have readily supported. Nevertheless the French in Louisberg had nothing to match this force. Their fortifications appeared strong enough, and they had five men o'war, as well as privateers and armed merchantmen to help defend the harbour. But they lacked men and supplies. Attempts to supply any more of these had now been checked by the British blockade. Hawke had destroyed a convoy bringing stores from Brest at Basque Roads, and in the Mediterranean a fleet under Admirals Osborne and Saunders had defeated a relief squadron from Toulon.

The attack on Louisbourg began at the end of May, when Boscawen came up from Halifax with a great fleet of some 160 sail; fighting ships and transports, carrying fourteen thousand troops. They anchored in Gabarus Bay, a broad inlet a few miles to the south of the harbour. It was in no way a surprise attack, and the French had prepared batteries overlooking the beaches.

Two days later the frigates and sloops moved in to bombard the shore. Then with Wolfe in command the ships' boats, loaded with light infantry and grenadiers, made for the beaches. It seemed a hazardous undertaking, - according to Wolfe, "a rash and ill-advised attempt", but it succeeded. Disregarding heavy fire, and even heavier surf the troops fought their way to a landing, although many of the boats were stove in and nearly a hundred men drowned.

The French defenders were soon pushed back, encampments were built, and notwithstanding difficulties due to bad weather, guns and ammunition were landed. For the next two months H.M.S. "Orford's" main role, along with the other men-of-war, was in the supply of "tents, ammunition, artillery and stores" for the use of the army. They also provided crews to help in the siege, particularly volunteers to dig trenches and mines under the walls of the town.

The attack was pressed forward, in spite of the difficulties due to the marshy ground, and in the face of heavy gunfire from the batteries, and the ships in the harbour. By the middle of July the besiegers were close to the citadel, and Wolfe had captured Lighthouse Point on the northern side of the entrance to the port. From here he could direct his artillery into the town and at the anchored ships, three of which were soon set on fire.

Boscawen now decided on a final stroke. On the twenty-fifth of July orders were sent to all the big ships to provide a barge and pinnace, manned and armed. These were despatched to join the squadron under Sir Charles Hardy, which lay close off the harbour mouth. That night, the flotilla of small boats, under the command of Captain Balfour of the fireship "Aetna", and of Captain John Laforey, rowed into the harbour. It was foggy, and they entered unseen. Laforey's men made for "Le Prudent", one of the men-of-war which they captured, but finding her aground set fire to her. Balfour's boats cut out the other, the "Bienfaisant", and towed her, under fire from the shore, to the top end of the harbour. It was brilliantly done, and there was now little to prevent the British ships from forcing their way into the port. The French defenders, short of ammunition and without hope of succour, decided to capitulate, and a few days later Boscawen led the British fleet in triumph into the port.

We have a description of the scene of destruction that met the British ships, from a book published in London later that year. This was "An Authentic Account of the Reduction of Louisbourg by A Spectator". That particular spectator was Valentine Nevill, Richard's purser aboard H.M.S. "Orford". Nevill wrote,

> "When our ships came into the Harbour, there was hardly any part of it which had not the appearance of Distress and Desolation, - Five or Six Ships sunk in one Place with their Mastheads peeping out of the Water, the stranded Hull of 'Le Prudent' on the

> muddy shoal on the other Side, burned down to the
> Water's Edge with a great deal of her Iron and Guns
> staring us in the face ..... and in the N.E. of the harbour
> little was to be seen but Masts, Yards and Rigging
> floating up and down, and Pieces of burned Masts,
> Bowsprits etc. driven to the Water's Edge, and some
> parts of the shore edged with Tobacco Leaves taken
> off some of the Ships that had been destroyed, - the
> whole a dismal Scene of total Destruction."

The news of the capture of Louisbourg caused predictable rejoicing back in England where the people were in need of a victory. French colours captured in the town, were paraded before the King, and carried triumphantly to St. Pauls. Captains Laforey and Balfour were promoted, the latter being given command of his prize the "Bienfaisant". With the fall of Louisbourg all of Cape Breton Island became part of the British Empire. Pitt gave orders for the defences of Louisbourg to be destroyed, and large numbers of the French inhabitants were to be shipped back to Farnce. There would never again be privateering from Cape Breton, against the British and American trade.

There had been victories on the other American fronts also. Forbes had suceeded in capturing Fort Dusquesne, and was building a new fort to be known as Fort Pitt, (and later Pittsburgh). An American force under Colonel Bradstreet had re-established control on Lake Ontario by capturing Fort Frontenac, and destroying the French fleet on the lake. But early in August news came of Abercromby's failure at Ticonderoga, where he had been driven back by Montcalm, and had suffered heavy losses. Amherst thereupon decided he must go the Abercromby's aid, and defend New York state against danger of a French advance.

It was now judged too late to move against Quebec. That would have to wait until the following year. The fleet was dispersed. Some were sent to Halifax under Philip Durell to be ready for an early campaign in 1759. The others including H.M.S. "Orford" returned to England. On the way they almost earned further laurels by the near capture of the homeward bound French fleet under Du Chauffault which had come out of the St. Lawrence. As they came into soundings in stormy weather the two fleets met. Boscawen had only three ships of the line, the "Bienfaisant", and three frigates with him, but he attacked the superior

French force of five of the line and one frigate. It seemed that Richard Spry might at last find himself in a fleet action, but as often happened in thick Atlantic weather, the French evaded them and escaped into Brest.

Nevertheless Boscawen and his company had every reason to feel content. They had earned their country's gratitude, and some of them made a handsome share of prize money. The Louisbourg operation had shown what soldiers and sailors working together could achieve. Wolfe was full of praise for the navy. Boscawen, he said, "had given all and even more than we could ask of him", and speaking of Sir Charles Hardy's close blockade, - "They rid out some very hard gales rather than leave an opening for the French to escape." Such co-operation augured very well for the following year, when the assault on Quebec could begin.

For Richard, like most of the other captains, it had been a quiet enough campaign. During much of the siege H.M.S. "Orford" had been lying at anchor in Gabarus Bay providing protection for the transports, although, with memories of the great gale of the year before, it must have been an anxious time, with increasing watchfulness against the weather as much as French frigates.

*Two frigates c. 1755*

# CHAPTER XI

## TO GLORY WE STEER

For Richard Spry and H.M.S. "Orford" it was a short winter at home, made busy by a refit in Plymouth Dock, and a spell of convoying 'the Trade', now east, now west, between the Hamoaze and Spithead. In January 1759 he was put under the command of Vice-Admiral Charles Saunders, with orders to get his vessel stored and manned ready for a foreign voyage of several months. None of Saunder's fleet was in any doubt as to where the voyage would lead them, for the transports were carrying troops under General Wolfe. They were about to embark on the second part of Pitt's plan for the conquest of Canada.

Saunders had taken Boscawen's place in command of the fleet with a squadron of ten ships of the line. The composition of smaller ships that were to accompany him reflected the task ahead, for in addition to several sloops there were three bomb vessels and three fire ships. This fleet had been preceded by another of battleships, frigates and troop transports under Charles Holmes, and there would be further additions under Lord Colville at Halifax. The fact that Saunders had been put in place of Boscawen in command of such a massive force was no reflection on the latter, who had taken charge of operations in the Mediterranean.

Charles Saunders was a fighting admiral, one of those taciturn and able characters so favoured by Anson. He had been with Anson on that famous voyage round the world fifteen years before, and had played an important part in Hawke's victory off Finisterre in 1747. On that occasion he was in command of H.M.S. "Yarmouth", and along with Saumarez had helped to stop the flight of the French ships. Richard knew Saunders well, for the latter had been a lieutenant aboard the "Exeter" when Spry had first joined the service.

Saunders got his fleet away in mid February. In spite of his wish to make a good passage they were unable to do so, for head winds and bad weather meant they did not arrive off Cape Breton until the end of April. They ran into thick ice floes surrounding Louisbourg, and after struggling vainly to break through into that harbour for another week, gave up and made for Halifax. Here Saunders was astonished to find Rear Admiral Durell still in port, for his orders required him to blockade the Gulf in St. Lawrence as early as possible. Durell explained that in view of the hard winter they had experienced, he had been waiting for news that the ice had cleared from the river. He was hastened to sea at once, but the damage had been done. Several French frigates had already slipped into the St. Lawrence with a score of transports carrying much needed stores for Quebec, as well as engineers and specialists in defence works. Among them was Louis Antoine Bougainville, a brilliant young French officer, who carried with him information concerning the English plan of attack, and gave Montcalm considerable help in preparing his defences.

The British intentions differed only in detail from those of the previous year. Amherst was in command of the land forces, and would make a thrust into Canada by way of Ticonderoga and the lakes. But the main attack would be up the river St. Lawrence against Quebec, with Wolfe in charge of the army and Saunders the navy.

Saunders now showed the quality of his leadership, and delighted the soldiers, by announcing that he intended to take the fleet all the way up the St. Lawrence. To give such an undertaking required considerable courage. None of the English captains had ventured far up the river, and Richard was one of the few who had been beyond Cape Gaspé at the entrance. It was known that they could expect fierce tides and strong head winds, and there would be narrow and tortuous passages through uncharted reefs and sand banks. Among British seamen the St. Lawrence had a reputation for dangers almost as formidable as Cape Horn. Many years before, in 1711, Admiral Walker had led an expedition against Quebec consisting of twenty men-of-war and 5,000 troops, an ill-conceived attempt that had ended with nearly half of his ships lost and 1,000 of his men drowned. Even the French, whose experience of the river's hazards was spread over two hundred years, considered it impossible to take anything bigger than a frigate as far as Quebec. They were confident now that the English would never attempt even that.

In spite of the difficulties and dangers, Saunders proceeded boldly and methodically. He had collected his enormous fleet of 170 sail at Louisbourg by early June. He was away by the fourth of that month, the smaller naval vessels leading the way, the others in their divisions with the transports among them. They passed through the Gulf of St.

*Map of St. Lawrence*

Lawrence with days of thick weather, and the winds blowing from every quarter.

Durell, making amends for his initial failure to seal the river, had gone ahead with frigates to capture the main islands and mark the channels. As they proceeded into the narrower parts of the estuary the ships' boats and smaller craft were busy taking soundings and laying buoys. Prominent in this work was Mr. James Cook, master of H.M.S. "Pembroke". It will be remembered that he had entered the navy by way of the lower deck only four years before and his talents had earned him rapid promotion. He had spent the past winter in Halifax under Captain John Simcoe, surveying and studying mathematics, and was now using his skills as a pilot and chartmaker. The work in the small boats went forward under difficulties. They were fired at by snipers from the banks, and at night were attacked by Indians. Nevertheless the fleet moved confidently on behind them, the captains of the merchant transports, many of whom were Americans, appearing particularly sanguine in their approach to the hazards.

Tides and currents presented the big ships with constant problems. Richard records a typical incident in his log,

"At 4 p.m. Mount Camille bore S.W. ½ S, 8 or 9 leagues. At 5 we Tackt to far over the N Shore we got into a Very Strong Tide or Current which set us to the N.W. And tho' at 8 o' clock a Breeze sprung up, which the Ship ought to have run at least three Knots an hour with, Yet would she not answer the helm, but kept her head to the N.N.W. forging in on the Monicouagan Shoal, so that I was oblig'd to hoist three Boats out to get her Head from the Shore and Tow her off. I wou'd therefore recommend it to everybody who sails up or down this River, constantly to keep the S Shore on board, and never to stand off to the Nward, even so far as Mid Channel."

On yet another occasion, when off the Pilgrims, - described as four little round islands stretching away about north-east from the southern shore,

..... "we were greatly Embarrased, for in falling into a quarter less 5 fathoms of water we did not know which way to Steer. However we soon deepen'd our water

and got safely through, tho' I believe we were very near
the Shoal which runs off from the Easternmost
Pilgrim. - Had we followed the Manuscript directions
found on board the "Alcide[1]" we should certainly
have kept in the best of the Channel."

Apart from the normal observations of courses, speed, the winds
and the sail that was carried, Richard's log is full of careful sailing
directions. Thus we are informed:

"Bird Islands are two small Islands about a quarter of
a mile distant from each other, the largest is very
remarkable with regard to its form, it appears like a
Large Square Building. Its sides seem to be quite
perpendicular and level on the Top, and white as a
Sheet by the Dung of Sea Birds."

Or again:

"In passing between Green and Red Island with found
a prodigious Strong Tide of Ebb, and great Rippling
for tho' we went at 8 knots and a half by Log, we scarce
went a Mile by the land. 'Tis necesary therefore to have
a fresh of Wind to carry you through against the Ebb."

In all this he found time for nature notes,

"This morning we saw numbers of Sea Lyons round
the ship which often go on shore on the Magdalen
Islands and are killed by the French Fishermen and
produce great quantities of Oyl. They have two large
Tusks in their Upper Jaw, bending downward which
are very good Ivory."

When they landed on Basque Island they found numbers of
ducks, geese and seals, "and the skeletons of many Hares which I
imagine had died by the severity of the Winter." On Apple Island, "were
a vast number of Gulls and Sea Mews which bred there, and we brought
on board great quantities of Eggs."

Day after day the armada moved up the swift flowing river,
anchoring when the tide was foul, weighing when it served, towing with

---

[1] See page 111.

their boats ahead when necessary. For most of the laborious passage H.M.S. "Orford" had been in the company of the Admiral, and Richard was delighted to be informed that for the attack on Quebec, Saunders' flag would be shifted into his ship. But then came a change of plans and Saunders went ahead aboard the "Stirling Castle", to see the first of the fleet pass safely through the Traverse.

The dreaded Traverse was the last great obstacle before they reached the Isle of Orleans and Quebec. It was an area of sandbanks and channels where the tide ripped through at speeds of up to nine knots, and where it was believed that deep laden vessels could not safely venture. The French had removed beacons showing where the channels lay, but Durell had captured a number of their pilots and had replaced the marks.

In the event, as so often happens with dreaded obstacles, the Traverse was passed easily enough. Wolfe and the troop transports were guided through first and by the twenty-seventh of June had seized the Isle of Orleans, and the battle for Quebec had begun. The ships of the line came up later, and Richard records the event as follows.

> "Moderate and fair Weather. At 10 this morning having a leading breeze, we Weigh'd by Signal in Order to pass through the Traverse, Four Sloops having been laid on the Edge of the Sand on each side to show us the Channel. Without this precaution 'twould be very difficult to keep the fairway through, the French having cut down all the Publick Marks."
> ..... "At half past Noon we anchored between the Isle of Orleans and Isle Madame in 7 fathoms Water, as did Admiral Durell and the rest of the Squadron."

Thus the Navy had achieved what many had believed would be impossible, without the loss of a ship. For all but a few of the 50 gun ships and frigates, the major part of the fleet had performed its main purpose. Henceforth the bigger vessels would be at anchor, in support of the army while it proceeded with the siege.

Thereafter the main work of the navy consisted of landing troops and stores at strategic points, providing covering fire and creating diversions, and escorting transports up and down the river. There were still some moments of excitement for the battleships. One was an easterly gale which drove into the exposed anchorage near the Isle Madame, and caused havoc among the transports, forcing some of them ashore. After that Saunders moved them to the more sheltered south-western end of the Isle of Orleans. The French made two attempts to destroy the shipping in this anchorage with fire ships. These were a complete failure, however, for the attacking vessels were fired too soon, and since something of the sort had been expected, boats from the warships towed them clear without difficulty.

For Richard, and no doubt for many of the other captains it was a period of inertia, and he notes that he spent much of the time fishing and shooting along the shores of the Isle of Orleans. Although the inhabitants had fled from the island there was a good deal of skirmishing from raiding parties. It was rarely safe to move far from the main defence points, and men were not allowed ashore except in armed bands.

Nevertheless Richard attempted to improve the diet of his crew by sending a ship's boat daily to the Isle of Orleans ......

"to gather Greens and all kinds of Garden Stuff,

Apples, Pease etc. for their Messmates. This was an excellent preventative against the Scurvy as each man took his turn to go on Shore, and was one would think the Sailors would be very fond of."

Alas for his hopes, for the inevitable happened.

"Even of this many of them soon grew tyred ..... in their wantonness setting the Houses and Barns on fire, which obliged us to put a stop to their Liberty. By which means great quantities of Refreshments perished, which would otherwise have been of infinite use to these ungovernable fellows."

Poor Richard was going through an unhappy time. He notes sadly,

"I am greatly disappointed at not having my Ship ordered up before the Town. Admiral Saunders having assured me he would hoist his flag on board the "Orford" during the Siege, notwithstanding which he ordered Six other ships without naming me."

There can be no doubt he was feeling pangs of professional jealousy at this neglect.

The French, having recovered from their shock at the arrival of the British fleet, were in a strong defensive position. The town of Quebec was built on the north bank of the St. Lawrence where it opened from a long narrow reach little more than a mile wide, and flowed past Cape Diamond into the great Basin of Quebec, an anchorage some four miles long by two miles wide. Here the river divided to go round the Isle of Orleans, the best channel being on the south side. The lower town of Quebec stretched along the waterside, a place of narrow streets and many wooden buildings. Behind it was the upper town of more substantial stone houses, including the citadel, churches and convents.

East of the town flowed the river St. Charles, and between this and another small river, the Montmorency, some eight miles away, the defenders had built long lines of batteries and entranchments. Here, and up the St. Lawrence above the town, General Montcalm had an army of some fifteen thousand men, and although many of them were peasants drafted into a militia, they far outnumbered the British troops. He also had a number of gun boats in the Basin, but his bigger vessels, store ships and frigates had been sent to anchorages far up the river, whence they could provide supplies of food and ammunition to Quebec.

In spite of the apparent strength of his position, however, Montcalm also had his problems. He was serving under the Governor General of Canada, the Marquis de Vaudreuil, a man with little military knowledge, and who shielded a number of corrupt officials. Supplies in the town were always short, and badly distributed so that the men in the French army were on smaller rations than those in the British forces. Moreover, although Montcalm had no doubts about their courage, he knew that most of his men lacked the training to face a professional army in an open battle. He therefore determined to keep them behind the defences, knowing that if he could hold out until October, the weather would force the British to retire.

Wolfe's first need was to establish strong positions on the Isle of Orleans, and at Point Levis on the south shore opposite the town. This was done within a few days by Brigadier Monckton, and from here the British were able to bombard the lower town, which was quickly reduced to a near ruin. More important, under such a bombardment, Saunders was able to slip a flotilla up the river past the French batteries. This daring manoeuvre was carried out at night by Captain Rous in the fourth rate H.M.S. "Sutherland", leading the frigate "Diana" (Captain Schomberg) and the sloop "Squirrel" (Captain Hamilton), as well as a number of transports. They took a flood tide and an easterly wind, and with the exception of the "Diana" were safely past before the defenders realised what was happening. The frigate went aground, and although she was refloated next morning she was badly damaged. Nevertheless this was a great tactical success, for now Wolfe could attack the French supply lines above the town and keep Montcalm in a state of indecision as to where the next blow would fall. Later more ships and barges were moved up, and the force was put under the command of Rear Admiral Holmes.

For Wolfe the real problem was how to bring the enemy to action, and he planned to do this by crossing the river Montmorency. The French had always believed that the North Channel, with reefs and shoals on both sides, was impassable to big ships. But a brilliant piece of pilotage by young John Jervis, the recently promoted commander of the sloop "Porcupine" showed that this was an error.

Wolfe thereupon moved some of his troops and artillery across to the undefended eastern bank of the Montmorency. Then on the thirty-first of July he mounted an attack on the entrenchments. H.M.S. "Centurion" and two armed transports ran in under the French batteries and landed some of the soldiers above the river, while others fought their way across a ford at the entrance. But the attack was a failure,

> "From some mistake in signal, or too great impetuosity, the Grenadiers advanced before a proper disposition was made for the attack", as Richard noted.

The result was a repulse with losses of some seven hundred men and it became clear that Quebec would not be easily taken from that side.

The siege dragged on, and for much of Richard's knowledge of what was happening he depended upon a friendly captain in Lascelle's regiment, who was posted on the southern point of the Isle of Orleans. From him he learned of the constant movement of troops and boats, the bombardments, the making of entrenchments, but also the savage guerilla war that was carried on with the French and Indians. Typical entries read,

> "This morning Three American Grenadiers were found sleeping in a Barn and Scalp'd by the Savages. Four men of a working party killed, and they had Time to Scalp but one ..... I cannot omit mentioning that a

favourite Sergeant, one Smythers was killed by a lurking rascall who was hid behind a Tree within about 10 yards of him ..... we find that in this petite Guerre the Enemy is equally dextrous in annoying us and taking care of themselves."

In return the attacking troops began to destroy the French crops, and to take their cattle. In the village of St. Joachim there was a particularly unpleasant reprisal,

"the parish priest at the head of the wretched peasants making a show of defence to save their Habitations were Inhumanly Butchered and the priest scalped by the order of Capt. Montgomery who commanded the party, the son praying for the Father's life and the Father for the sons, alike unheard. The General showed his Disapprobation of such inhuman proceedings by a Subsequent Order to Capt. Gorham wherein he gives positive Orders to spare all when the opposition he meets with ceases, and concludes that Cruelty is the most distinguishing Characteristic of Cowardice."

At the end of August, Wolfe was a sick man, and in something of a dilemma. There was little more than a month of campaigning left, and although Amherst was pushing on towards Montreal there was no hope of help from that direction. He still thought that an attack on the entrenchments at Beaupré offered the best solution, but when his brigadiers and Admiral Saunders proposed making it above the town he agreed. Their suggestion was that it should be some miles up the river, but he made the final decision that it should be at the Anse du Foulon, only a little way above the town.

The assault began on the night of the twelfth of September, and it was brilliantly conceived and brilliantly executed. Full use was made of the mobility granted by the use of the ships. As a diversion Saunders brought his big vessels into action, moving them into the Basin of Quebec to bombard the batteries below the town, and to create the impression that here was the main attack. Up the river a small flotilla under Holmes had been wearing out part of the French army, led by De Bougainville, by keeping them marching to and fro to stave off threatened landings.

Finally from transports up the river where men had been hidden in the holds, from Brigadier Monckton's encampments on the southern shore and from those on the Pointe d'Orleans, several thousand troops came crowding through the darkness. It was Rear Admiral Charles Holmes' task to direct these to their landing, an operation he described as "the most hazardous and difficult I was ever engaged in."

This too succeeded brilliantly, and soon the troops were scaling the steep cliffs up what were little better than goat tracks. Admiral Saunders in his letter to Mr. Secretary Pitt wrote,

> "the difficulty of gaining the Top of the Hill is scarce credible. It was very steep in its Ascent and high, and had no Path where two could go abreast; but they were obliged to pull themselves up by the Stumps and Boughs of Trees that covered the Declivity."

Up went the light infantry, and by dawn Wolfe had safely mustered his army of four and half thousand men on the Heights of Abraham. The surprise was complete, for the French had considered such a feat impossible and had failed to prepare a proper defence. Moreover with the danger of attack at several points, Montcalm had been compelled to dissipate his strength and he was now forced from behind his defences with an army hardly bigger than Wolfe's.

The battle that followed was short but fierce, and was finally settled by a bayonet charge from the British troops that sent the French into flight. The casualties were heavy, about five hundred British and fifteen hundred French, among them Generals Wolfe and Montcalm. Richard's note on the end of the siege reads,

> "The Enemy, disheartened by their Defeat, and in Want of Provisions of all kinds, having made a show of Defence for a few days, Capitulated and gave Quarters to the English Army in Quebec for the Winter, which finished a Campaign equally glorious to the General who conducted it and the Army who served under him."

By now Richard was up before the town in the Basin of Quebec, for if it had not surrendered, Saunders intended a full scale bombardment. The admiral now set about getting his ships clear and out of the river before the ice came. Captain James Douglas of the

"Alcide" was sent home with despatches of the victory, which earned him a knighthood and further promotion. Rear Admiral Durell and Charles Holmes sailed soon after for England in charge of the bigger vessels, while those from the American stations returned with Lord Colville to Halifax.

H.M.S. "Orford" was kept back, for Saunders had chosen her for a final distinction. Although the campaign had been won, the war in Canada was not yet over. There was still a large French force at Montreal, and there were several enemy frigates a long way up the river. Saunders thought that these might be brought down either to escape to France, or to attack the garrison in Quebec, and Richard was left in charge of a small squadron of eight frigates and sloops, to protect the port.

Saunders' last official orders before he sailed on the eleventh of October were for "Orford" to remain there until the twentieth, or as long as possible, and to destroy the French squadron if it came down. Brigadier Monckton who had been badly wounded in the battle was left in Richard's care and was to be taken to New York aboard H.M.S. "Fowey", when the squadron sailed. Richard remained in the Basin without outstanding incidents until the end of the month, when he decided he could stay no longer. Then with the "Medway", "Fowey" and "Lizard", and a convoy of merchant vessels, he sailed leaving behind four sloops and some seven thousand troops in Quebec.

They were away just in time, for although they passed the Traverse in moderate, clear weather, the following day it began to snow. Thereafter the "Orford's" log records successive days with gales of wind and blizzards, in which they drove down the St. Lawrence under reefed canvas. Most of the transports lost touch with her on the way down, but they were by then in little danger from the French.

The passage back which took so long on the way up was completed in four days. At the entrance of the Gulf Richard despatched H.M.S. "Fowey", and set course for England, still in company with H.M. ships "Medway" and "Lizard". They anchored in Spithead on the twenty-first of November. "After a very favourable passage with nothing remarkable happening ...... Thus happily ended our Quebec Expedition."

It was indeed a happy ending, not just for that Canadian expedition, but for a whole series of successes, in what became known as the "Year of Victories". And the final and perhaps most momentous had taken place the night before, while "Orford" had been racing up the

Channel on the wings of a north-west gale. That had been Hawke's crushing blow at the French fleet in Quiberon Bay, a victory that brought an end to the threat of invasion. Although Richard missed the battle by several days, he knew most of the men and ships engaged.

Events leading up to Quiberon Bay had begun in the early part of the year when the French War Minister, the Duc de Choiseul decided that the only way of taking the pressure off Canada, and perhaps settling the war at a stroke, was the invasion of England. It was the old strategy that has been planned time and again, even to the present century. Invasion barges were massed in the Channel ports, and an army of 20,000 men made ready on the banks of the River Schelde to be launched against the East coast. Another massive force was collected in Brittany with the intention of descending on the West coast of Scotland. As a diversion, a third attack would be made on Northern Ireland.

The success of Choiseul's plan depended on the French naval forces from Toulon and Brest joining together to gain control of the Channel and provide cover, first for the invasion of Scotland, then by way of the North Sea to assist the landing on the coast of Essex. To prevent this Boscawen had been sent to blockade Toulon, while Hawke was keeping watch off Brest.

In August after several months on the blockade, Boscawen was forced to retire to Gibraltar to replenish and refit his ships. The French admiral, De La Clue saw his opportunity to slip out of Toulon with twelve ships of the line, and escape through the Straits. They reached the entrance with a fair wind, a thick haze, and night coming on. Without doubt they would have escaped into Atlantic and thence towards Brest but for Richard's old frigate, H.M.S. "Gibraltar". She had been left on patrol, and seeing the ships looming through the dark, hauled up for the Rock, firing guns as she went.

Boscawen had most of his ships out of action, sails unbent and their crews ashore. Yet within a couple of hours, by prodigious effort, they were out at sea and in pursuit of the French who were still being shadowed by the "Gibraltar". They caught up with part of La Clue's fleet on the following day, and a running fight developed. It ended when the French admiral fled into Lagos Bay and sought the protection of Portuguese neutrality. But Sir Edward decided that four men o' war were worth the risk of offending an old ally. He sailed in and destroyed two, and took two as prizes.

One of Richard's old friends, Matthew Buckle (still Boscawen's flag captain aboard H.M.S. "Namur") distinguished himself, as did

Captain Bentley who captured the "Temeraire". But the greatest glory went to Boscawen who had handled the whole affair with notable skill and determination.

With the Toulon squadron destroyed or sheltering in Spanish ports, the French hopes centred on the Brest fleet, still blockaded by Hawke. This was kept inactive until mid November when Hawke was driven off station by a westerly gale. De Conflans, the French Admiral, escaped, and made southwards intending to pick up the army waiting for him in the Morbihan. But Hawke went in pursuit and in a memorable battle fought in the darkness among the reefs and tide rips of Quiberon Bay, destroyed a large part of the French fleet. Two were sunk, two captured, others burned or driven ashore, and the rest scattered into various refuges.

This was the victory that rounded off that wonderful year. There had been other notable ones in India and the West Indies, as well as in Europe at Minden, and in Canada where Amherst had taken Ticonderoga and Fort Niagara. But essentially it had been the Navy's year. People safe on shore recognised it. In their churches they gave thanks to God who "had given such signal successes to our arms both by sea and land". And in the theatres and in the streets they sang "Hearts of Oak" Mr. David Garrick's new song

"Come cheer up my lads, 'tis to glory we steer,
To add something new to this wonderful year."

# CHAPTER XII

## THE LONG BLOCKADE

If Richard ever felt that fame had eluded him in that glorious year he was given another chance to attain it early in 1760. A signal from Boscawen sent him hurrying out of Plymouth Sound at the end of February, taking with him two frigates H.M.S. "Aurora" under Captain Samuel Scott, and H.M.S. "Minerva" under Alexander Hood. They were ordered to cruise off the southern coast of Ireland to intercept a French squadron expected down the Irish Sea.

This squadron was the third force, which had momentarily vanished, and was all that was left of De Choiseul's grand design for the invasion of the British Isles. It was the diversionary part of the scheme and consisted originally of five frigates carrying several thousand troops. It was commanded by Monsieur Thurot, the noted privateer captain who had evaded the British blockade outside Dunkirk during a gale in the previous October, and, having made his way across the North Sea to Gothenburg, spent some time refitting. Thereafter, he sailed early in December bound towards the north of Scotland, and the subsequent adventures of his squadron show once more the difficulties of maintaining control of the sea at that time.

The news that Thurot was out created great alarm in English coastal shipping. He held a considerable reputation as a bold seaman, and no one was sure of his intentions. Groups of cruisers went looking for him but he had faded from view. During that period he spent a month at anchor in the Faeroes before moving on, then being driven into the remote Sound of Islay by a series of westerly gales. Here he remained for several more weeks effecting repairs and restoring his men, for it had been a hard voyage, and two of his ships had gone missing.

At last, in mid February, he appeared at his destination in Belfast Lough. Here he landed at Carrickfergus, and having captured the port without much effort, besieged the crumbling castle. This was garrisoned by a Lieutenant Colonel Jennings and a small army of recruits. These fought gallantly enough, and it is said that when their ammunition ran out they defended the walls by hurling stones and rubble. Inevitably the castle surrendered, for Thurot was more than ready to grant honourable terms. By now he had learned of the French defeat at Quiberon and knew that the great invasion plan had failed. So having replenished his victuals he determined to make for France, and headed down the Irish Sea.

There on the last day of February he was intercepted by three British frigates, H.M.S. "Pallas" and H.M.S. "Brilliant" led by Captain Elliot in H.M.S. "Aeolus". Each singled out one of the enemy and within two hours Thurot was killed, and all his ships were taken. Poor Thurot had behaved in exemplary fashion throughout, but had met with misfortune after misfortune. His defeat was celebrated with rejoicing throughout England, out of all proportion to the danger he had ever presented.

Meanwhile Richard Spry was quartering the sea a few miles to the south unaware of how narrowly he had missed glory once more. Only when he put into Kinsale early in March did he learn that it was all over, and fresh orders had been sent him to join the fleet in the Bay of Biscay. There followed a spring and summer, patrolling the west coast of France from Brest to Bordeaux, for although the French naval strength had been shattered for the time, they still had numerous privateers swarming out of their harbours to attack British trade. There was also a small squadron to be kept penned in the Pertuis Breton, off La Rochelle. Richard was among old friends again, and even if the work was monotonous, it was exacting enough, much of it being performed close to the land, with intricate pilotage in rock stewn waters. After six months of this Richard was given a spell ashore to recover from an attack of scurvy, and his place aboard "Orford" was taken by Captain Thomas Graves.

Thomas Graves was a fellow Cornishman, son of a rear admiral and with many connections in the navy. He had seen a good deal of active service, having fought aboard H.M.S. "Monmouth" as a Lieutenant, with both Anson and Hawke in the two battles off Finisterre in 1747. In later years, as Admiral Lord Graves he served in the American wars. Some blamed him then for the failure to relieve Cornwallis at Yorktown, an event that precipitated the loss of the American colonies. But now as temporary commander of H.M.S. "Orford" he had better fortune, for he made a prize of a large French vessel within a few weeks of taking over.

At the end of May 1761, Richard was back aboard the "Orford", restored to health, and glad to be once more at sea. He was sent immediately to join Matthew Buckle keeping a close blockade of Brest in H.M.S. "Namur". The meeting was a sad one, however, for a few weeks earlier their much-loved Admiral Boscawen had died of typhoid. Boscawen's death at the early age of fifty was a severe loss to the service. He had served with distinction throughout many years and had provided an example for men to follow in the hard times to come. Now his body was taken to his family home in the small village of St. Michael Penkivel in Cornwall, where his memorial in the parish church makes a fitting tribute. It tells that "his concern for the interest, and unwearied attention to the health of all under his command, softened the necessary exaction of duty, and the rigours of discipline."

Within a few days of "Orford's" arrival off Brest, H.M.S. "Namur" departed, leaving Richard senior officer of the squadron. He had under him six ships of the line, two frigates, and several small sloops and cutters[1]. His immediate object was to keep watch, and prevent the escape of a French squadron of equal strength that was lying in the Rade de Brest. The resources of the French were such that within eighteen months of heavy defeats they had been able to bring large vessels into commission again.

The task facing Richard and his squadron was not an easy one. They were carrying out that close blockade of Brest and the west coast of France, begun by Hawke, and continued by the navy throughout many decades of later wars. The harbour of Brest lies within a bight of the sea known as Iroise, the port and its roadstead being completely sheltered by high land. Entrance to the harbour can only be made through a narrow inlet called the Goulet de Brest. Within that shelter the French could build, fit out and maintain their fleet until the right conditions allowed them to slip out to sea.

Outside the harbour, conditions for the blockading fleet were full of hazards. The prevailing west wind made a lee shore of the entire coast. Here there were widely scattered islands, reefs and shallows, made double dangerous by frequent mists and racing tides. Yet the blockade required that the ships should be close in so that they might attack those wishing to come out, or search neutrals wishing to enter. If they were kept far off French vessels could easily escape by one of the channels behind the reefs, either to the north by way of the Chenal du

[1] See appendix II.

Four, or to the south by way of the Toulinguet passage.

The practice was to keep the big men of war well off-shore, with an inshore squadron of frigates in the Iroise, and a chain of connecting vessels between. Richard's rendezvous position in H.M.S. "Orford" varied between nine and twenty-four miles west of Ushant according to the weather. Three of his ships lay off Audierne Bay watching movements to the south, while in easterly weather others cruised off the Black Rocks close to Ushant. At one time his frigates "Aeolus" and "Niger" were lying at anchor for weeks on end to the south east of St. Matthew point, from which position they could observe directly into the entrance of Brest harbour.

It was a cat and mouse affair, and for most of the ships entailed long periods of beating to and fro or being hove-to. From time to time they would break away to intercept distant sails, to stop and examine one of the neutrals which as Richard noted "swarmed around Ushant".

Occasionally there were interesting incidents, such as that described in one of his reports to the Admiralty. The wind was easterly and the weather thick, so H.M.S. "Arethusa" had come to an anchor near the Toulinguet Channel. She lay there for two days, Captain Vane hoping he might pick up a vessel creeping out of Brest. On the third morning they made out a large brig close under the land, and the first lieutenant went off in one of the boats to intercept. He found her to be a Spaniard, and received some valuable information on the state of the squadron lying in Brest Roads. When the boat tried to return however, a thick fog had settled, and they made their way guided by a gun fired every half hour by the "Arethusa". Suddenly there loomed up over them a large vessel which proved to be a French frigate. The boat was ordered alongside but they made off into the fog, and after rowing about for several more hours regained their own ship. The fog did not lift for another twenty four hours, and although a search was then made for the French vessel, she had got clear away.

For the most part however the blockade was a wearisome business which wore out ships and men, causing frayed gear and frayed tempers. They suffered all the perils and discomforts of seafaring without actually going anywhere. For Richard Spry there was the constant worry of maintaining his ships, and the fear that the French might come out and escape him because theirs were clean and his were foul. For the crews there was sickness and boredom to be overcome, and the only hope of relief was when each ship was sent in turn to Plymouth for a short refit, but without leave. Otherwise, stores came out in small victuallers which brought fresh water, live cattle and sheep, beer, butter and cheese, wood and coal, and an occasional relief seaman.

It is difficult for us to appreciate the difficulties and hardships of that long blockade, with its lack of comfort and lack of rest. It must have been one of the hardest schools for seamen anywhere. Its chief purpose was to prevent the invasion of these islands by keeping apart the French fleets, and at the same time stop supplies from reaching their colonies. But it had another profound and lasting effect on the British Navy: it raised generations of officers and men certain of their ability to outfight any others in the world. Most of all it made them eager for action, for they welcomed anything that would bring the war and the wearisome blockade to an end.

Richard's immediate superior was commodore Augustus Keppel, then lying with part of the fleet in Belle Isle Roads, off the entrance to Quiberon Bay. Keppel had just succeeded in capturing Belle Isle after a combined operation between army and navy. It had been a brilliant success against strong defences, and was part of Pitt's design to bottle up the French fleet, and at the same time provide him with a strong bargaining piece when the war should end. Moreover, the seizure of such a large island only a few miles off their coast had been a severe blow to French pride.

Belle Isle's chief asset was its strategic position. It had only one real harbour, the little river port of Le Palais, a walled town protected by a strong fortress. But outside there was a good anchorage for the big ships, well-sheltered from westerly gales. Here Keppel in H.M.S. "Valiant" lay at anchor, ready to assist Spry off Brest, or Sir Thomas Stanhope with the other blockading squadron off Rochefort.

Commodore Keppel was well known to Richard who had served him when he sailed to Virginia in the "Gibraltar" five years before. Keppel was an attractive character, for although an aristocrat he was amiable and courteous to those under him. His early seafaring experiences had been varied and arduous, when as a midshipman of fifteen he had taken part in Anson's world voyage. In 1759 he had shared in the capture of Goree in French West Africa, and had further distinguished himself at Hawke's victory at Quiberon. Now, in 1761, there had been the capture of Belle Isle, which would be followed the following year by another success at the siege of Havana.

Meanwhile, there was the business of blockade. The letters between Keppel and Richard are friendly and full of the usual confidence in their ability to handle to French if they got to sea. It was

Keppel's opinion that when the time was right Admiral Blenac with the fleet from Brest would slip out and make for Rochefort hoping to catch the British squadron there in a pincer movement. "If they come near Belle Isle," he says, "we will have a good play, as I think you will if Monsieur Blenac calls upon you on his way out." Richard agrees, concluding "that 7 or 8 sail will be enough to beat any squadron that the French dare to send against us."

It was part of Richard's duty to send regular reports to the Commodore on what he could discover of the state of the squadron in Brest, as well as an account of the movement of his own ships. Mixed with these are comments on the sailing qualities of the vessels. The "Royal William", a second rate under Captain Hugh Pigot is "much the best sailing ship in the squadron, either by the wind or large". On the other hand the "Prince Frederick" sails "bitter bad". There are good-natured jokes about some of the captains. Thus we hear that Captain James Gambier ("my friend Jemmy", Richard calls him) is inordinately proud of his new ship H.M.S. "Burford". But, says Richard, "every vessel in the squadron can beat the "Burford".

Occasionally we get a hint of minor excitements. A French privateer is sighted of Ushant and H.M.S. "Hampton Court" sent in chase, with every prospect of catching her. But she comes back empty-handed;

> "had I sent anybody but Scrope after her we should
> certainly have had her, but he is so unlucky a Rogue
> that 'tis impossible for him to meet with success in
> anything. After he got her under his guns the wind
> dyed away, and she (the privateer) having thrown hers
> overboard she left him very fast."

It was not all misfortunes. Captain Hotham, on his way to Plymouth for a refit, picked up a smuggler off Rame Head and took her in as a prize. A few days later three of the squadron intercepted a French merchantman from the West Indies loaded with a valuable cargo of coffee and indigo.

Early in August the blockading squadrons were brought to a state of extreme anticipation by the news that a number of French ships, led by the well known "Courageux" of 74 guns was coming from San Domingo and making for Brest. Here was a chance to strike a blow and earn a fortune. Week after week they watched, and then came news that Richard notes, "brought all my golden dreams to an end." The

"Courageux" was captured by an old companion Robert Faulkner, almost by accident. Captain Faulkner, in command of H.M.S. "Bellona" and accompanied by the frigate "Brilliant" under Captain Loggie, met with "Courageux" and two smaller vessels off the Portuguese coast. In a fiercely fought action all three French vessels were taken.

From then on we begin to note an inevitable decline in morale in Richard's squadron. Many of the ships were reporting outbreaks of scurvy. The "Essex" had seventy men sick and with little hope of recovery. Gambier not a man given to exaggeration wrote that he was short of water, his main mast was sprung his crew was falling down with scurvy. Others made similar reports, and Richard expressed his concern to Keppel. He was particularly worried about the unfortunate Scrope of the "Hampton Court".

> "Yesterday my surgeon was sent for to poor Scrope
> who is extremely ill and reduced to a mere skeleton by
> the Flux. The Surgeons are all of the Opinion that he
> has no chance for his life, but getting him on shore as
> soon as possible."

Scrope did indeed nearly get on shore, but not in the way he would have chosen. For that very day, with the wind in the east, the big ships had closed the land. The wind then dropped clean away and they were in danger of drifting on to the rocks, so that they were forced to lower their boats, and tow for a day and a night until the breeze came back to save them. That was a hard task for all hands, and particularly the many who were sick.

Keppel could offer little sympathy to all this. As he wrote back "If you have any Philosophy you must make use of it, and comfort yourself as I do, that Time must put an end to all things."

In fact relief was close at hand for Richard. It was overdue, for he was a sick man himself. His ship had been at sea continuously for months. She was short of stores, and her deck and upper works were in a poor state. In October Matthew Buckle arrived in the "Namur", with orders for him to return to Plymouth for a refit. There he received a letter from John Cleveland. The Admiralty were well pleased with his vigilant conduct off Ushant, and they had appointed him to a new vessel, H.M.S. "Mars" of 74 guns.

There was a short and hectic stay in Plymouth, re-commissioning the "Mars" and getting her ready for sea. Richard had

particular cause to feel pleased in that almost the entire crew of the
"Orford", some of whom had now sailed with him for seven years,
requested permission to transfer to the new ship. He was allowed to take
only a hundred of them, but the fact that so many wished to go is a fair
indication of his popularity.

By the beginning of December he was away to the westward
again to join the Brest squadron. He immediately ran into bad weather,
for which the ship was ill prepared. Many of her sails were old, having
been taken from other vessels, because the new ones were still being
made in Plymouth sail loft. Several of these blew out in the gale, and he
had to borrow again from other ships in the squadron. Moreover,
Richard was again a sick man. While in Plymouth he had written to the
Admiralty to say; "I am at present so ill that I cannot hold the pen in my
hand, but am in hopes that a few days confinement and care will make
me fit for duty again, tho' I am afraid the Scurvy has got too fast a hold
on me to be soon eradicated."

Off Ushant he found that Commodore Keppel had come north
to strengthen the blockade for it was believed that Blenac was ready to
come out. However, the stay there was a short one. A furious westerly
gale drove them off the station and they were forced to run to Torbay
for shelter.

The long blockade had made Torbay of considerable import-
ance to the fleet. True there were but few facilities, with a fishing village
with a quay at Brixham and a boat landing at Torre[1], but there was a
vast bay into which ships could safely run and anchor. Stores could be
easily obtained from Plymouth, for the victuallers could sail from there
in a day with a west wind.

While the squadron gathered in Torbay, Keppel received orders
to proceed to Portsmouth. Pitt had been working hard to prevent an
alliance between France and Spain, but his hopes had been ended when
the two nations formed a "Family Compact". Now he felt that the navy
could cope with their combined fleet, so in December he declared war
on Spain.

Keppel's recall was to help in the preparations now being made
for an attack on Spanish possessions in the West Indies, and it resulted
in Richard's appointment as commodore of the Brest squadron. At that
time the position of commodore was a post, not a rank. The holder of
the position was in effect an acting, temporary rear admiral, but at the

---

[1] Torquay, then only a row of cottages, owed its growth to the comings and goings of the
Navy during the blockade.

end of the particular appointment he would return to being a captain again. Nevertheless for Richard it was a clear step up, and although he was "a commodore without a captain" (that is, he was still in sole command of H.M.S. "Mars") he was entitled to the privileges of the post, and to hoist a broad pendant at his masthead.

The promotion came at a most difficult time. He had still not completely recovered from the scurvy. There was trouble with some of the stemhead fastenings of the "Mars" which had drawn apart in the recent gale. Worst of all the whole squadron was desperately short of stores. In spite of the fact that the victuallers had only a short run to leeward, they had failed to arrive. Urgent demands were made for all manner of necessities, to Mr. Ommaney, head of the Victualling Office in Plymouth, but he could only send distressed excuses. The truth was he was unable to get the masters of the vessels out of the shelter at the Cattewater.

> "They are such a set of Shocking men, making one excuse after another, (he wrote) ..... the Duty of the whole Navy would not give me the Trouble and Vexation and Disappointment as a few of the perverse Masters of Transports who seem to me to disregard Duty, to lye in the harbour and get their Wages for nothing else."

Nevertheless, Richard's orders required that he should get the squadron back on to the station off Ushant as soon as the weather allowed. On the twenty-first of January, the wind shifted to the northeast and he was away at once, although still without the supplies he needed for both ships and men. On passage he met with some devastating news. The wind that had brought the squadron over from Torbay had allowed Admiral Blenac with seven frigates to slip out of Brest, and away across the Atlantic. They were laden with troops and reputed to be bound for Martinique, then under siege by Admiral Rodney. It seemed that all those painful months of blockade had been thrown away[1]. Now all that Richard could do was to despatch his fastest frigate, the "Aquilon", to the West Indies to warn Rodney and Holmes of the French escape. Then leaving a few vessels to watch outside Brest, he brought the rest of the squadron back to Plymouth.

---

[1] In the event the French fleet came too late to save Martinique which was captured by Rodney and Sir James Douglas in February, 1762, before Blenac's arrival.

It was a piece of unbelievably bad fortune that this should happen at the beginning of Richard's post of commodore. He knew that the Admiralty would attach no blame, for his orders had mentioned the possibility of it happening. Nevertheless he was aware that there would be criticism in some quarters, and it was certain that the general public would raise an outcry[2]. He remembered how they had done that to an admiral as famous as Hawke after De Conflans escaped from Brest in 1759, and even while Hawke was fighting the desperate battle in Quiberon Bay voices had been raised against him. Nevertheless Richard's despatch to the Secretary of the Admiralty shows something of the depth of his misery over the incident.

> "I should make but a bad advocate in my own favour, and if I knew myself guilty of any error I would not wish to hide it. - That my Character will be tore to pieces by the generalty of the people of England I am too sensible of, for this has ever been the lot of the unfortunate. But if I am not utterly condemned by their Lordships it will greatly alleviate the distress and anxiety I cannot help feeling on this occasion, tho' I have not the least thing to reproach myself with, except my ill luck."

The Admiralty response to this pathetic letter was to put H.M.S. "Mars" into Plymouth Dock for repairs to the hull, and to give Richard several weeks leave. The spell ashore allowed him to recover in body and spirit. But he was saddened by the news that Anson, who had been First Lord of the Admiralty for the past ten years, had been taken ill. Anson had been one of the guiding hands of the British navy for as long as Richard could remember. He had been responsible for many improvements in construction and design that had helped to make it victorious. His humanity had helped to remove some of the grossest abuses in the treatment of crews, and his courage had become a model for the entire service. But in April the old sailor made his last voyage from London to Bath, where he died a few weeks later.

The death of the Admiral meant the end of patronage for Richard. His former commanders had gone, Warren, Boscawen, now

---

[2] The eminent historian of the Seven Years War, Sir Julian Corbett blamed Spry, saying that Blenac had "given him the slip". But even eminent historians sometimes make unfair comment, and Corbett was misinformed over the sequence of events.

Anson, and henceforth there would be different voices in the Admiralty. He was not long in noticing the differences. When "Mars" was ready for sea, Richard was ordered to sail for Belle Isle and take command of the squadron watching Quiberon Bay. In his reply Richard allowed himself an uncharacteristic complaint;

> "after the many disagreeable Services that I have been employed on during the whole course of this War, both in America and England, I flattered myself I might have some chance for a cruise, my ship being perfectly Clean and reputed to sail very well, and many of the Enemies ships both France and Spanish being now on their passage home."

The response was a rebuke from My Lords both swift and uncompromising. He was informed that he was not expected to question his orders, for he was not in a position to judge requirements. "Growl you may, but go on you must" is an old sea saying, and Richard, having growled, went, aggrieved no doubt in the belief that other more favoured captains were given cruises. By the middle of June he was off Belle Isle once more on the blockade watching the coast from Penmarch'h to the Isle D'Yeu and prepared to ward off any attack on the island by French forces. He had eight big vessels to maintain, as well as numerous sloops and cutters, and in addition was required to support a second squadron under Peter Dennis, which was blockading Basque Roads.

The work for the commodore was not greatly different to that he had known off Ushant. There was a constant shuttle of vessels bringing food and supplies from Plymouth and Cork. Throughout the hot summer the ships were in need of fresh water, much of which was obtained from rain water tanks on Belle Isle. But the supply was inadequate, and the water from Belle Isle was notorious for inducing the colic.

With the greater part of the French navy off the seas, the biggest task for the squadron was to put a stop to the coasting trade. This was carried on by small vessels in and out of the little ports of Vannes, Nantes and Le Croisic, bringing food to the naval base at Port Louis. As a humanitarian gesture French fishing boats were left unmolested as long as they were fishing, although on occasion a "chasse marée" would try to break the blockade by carrying cargo, and was therefore liable to arrest.

Many of Richard's letters to the Chevalier Redmond the local commandant at Vannes, concern such incidents. These are couched in most amiable terms. A fishing boat has been seized by a privateer and the captain's son held to ransom. Richard promises to get the boy released and any money paid will be returned. His reward is a gift from the Chevalier of a supply of fruit, vegetables and wine. On another occasion he assures Redmond that provisions sent by the Bishop of Vannes for the poor peasants of Belle Isle will be fairly distributed among them.

Not only was this limited warfare in keeping with the eighteenth century attitudes, but the truth was that many people were weary of fighting. Peace would not be signed for another nine months, but meanwhile both sides seemed to be taking a more relaxed view of the struggle. The Chevalier offers to send any luxuries needed from the mainland. Richard replies, "If I should hereafter have occasion for any small trifle from the Continent by way of a present for a fair lady, or a few hampers of best Claret for my own use, I shall take advantage of your friendly offer."

The reference to a fair lady is interesting, for it shows a different aspect of Richard's somewhat puritanical nature. It may of course, have been simply to impress a Frenchman. Meanwhile he met a request from Chevalier Redmond for a few English books to read. Brigadier Lambert, the Governor of Le Palais provided a copy of Hume's "Essays", and Richard added a note, "I have had the good fortune to get Dr. Young's 'Night Thoughts' from one of my Gentlemen. I also beg leave to present you with a Book of Dr. Youngs, since published.".

Such philosophical works would seem heavy going for a Frenchman, unless the name Redmond shows that the Chevalier was of old English or Irish emigré stock. With these pleasantries went exchanges of prisoners, and permits for islanders to leave for the mainland.

One is aware that Richard's earlier attitudes towards the French, once a mixture of dislike and disdain have undergone a change. He has learned to appreciate some of their virtues, and he shows increasingly friendly feelings towards them. However, there came a flurry of more warlike activities in the middle of summer, largely directed against Spain. The Spaniards had invaded our old ally Portugal, and many of the seasoned troops from Belle Isle were required to hold them back.

Richard's squadron was closely involved in this operation. In a letter to his friend Captain Dennis, he writes,

"I have been so busy for this three or four days past embarking and disembarking Troops with their Equipages, Horses, Whores etc. etc., that I was never so much fatigued in my whole life."

On the same day he wrote a more formal account to his Commander in Chief, Sir Edward Hawke.

"I have embarked with the utmost expedition in my power all the Troops, Artillery with their Horses, Dragoons, Regimental Horses, Stores and Lumber destined for Lisbon on board the Transports ..... and give me leave to assure you Sir that I attended myself on the Beach from daylight till dark during the three days of embarking.

Permit me now Sir to wish you all the Success and honor which you are so justly entitled to from your great Merit, and let me interest you to believe me when I assure you that I should deem myself extremely happy to have the honor of making one of your Sea Fleet, and I hope that you will join with me in thinking that the Mars is too good a Ship to be pinned down to an anchor in Belle Isle Road ..... I can promise you a tolerable Clean Ship, constantly hogged twice a week, not ill manned, reputed to sail well, and her Captain will think it the highest honor to do his duty under your Eye."

In spite of this flowery letter, Richard's hopes were not fulfilled. The main thrust of war had shifted to other seas. In June a lightning attack on Newfoundland had been made by four French men of war which escaped the blockade. They captured St. Johns, but were soon driven off by the Halifax squadron under Lord Colville. In the West Indies the great fortress of Havana was under siege, by a combined force, with the navy under Pocock and Keppel. A British expedition was under way in the East Indies that would shortly result in the taking of Manilla. Spain which had entered the war late, was paying dearly for her adventure.

In August Spry's squadron was recalled from the blockade, with the clear intention of sending them as reinforcements to America. Richard was relieved as captain of the "Mars", although he continued to live aboard and hoist his flag in her as commodore. But even as they were about to sail from Plymouth, news came of the fall of Havana, and the wrangling over terms of peace which had been going on for so long between London and Paris came to an end. In a few more weeks preliminaries were signed, and the Seven Years War was all but over.

For Britain it was the end of what was probably the most successful war she has fought. For Richard Spry it was to be the end of his service as a fighting captain.

# EPILOGUE FOR AN ADMIRAL

The war which Richard Spry had just survived had been "long, bloody and expensive" but it established Britain firmly as an imperial power, controlling vast areas of the world, in North America and in India. Yet, as ever, when peace came the forces that had made victory possible were soon cut down. Spry was one of the fortunate ones, for he was sufficiently senior to be saved the indignity of being sent home on half pay.

He remained as commodore, with a captain under him, in H.M.S. "Mars" for another year, taking her once more across the Atlantic, first to Newfoundland, and then to Halifax, Nova Scotia. Here he lay for the winter of 1762 as Commander-in-Chief of the American station. The following summer he went south to Port Royal in Jamaica to join Admiral Keppel, fresh from the victorious campaign against Havana. His last voyage in H.M.S. "Mars" took him back to Portsmouth carrying Keppel's despatches.

There followed a curious interval in command of the Royal Yacht "Fubbs" based on Harwich and Greenwich. This was something of a sinecure, for "Fubbs" was only used occasionally to take royal personages to and from Holland. She was a beautiful little vessel, less than 150 tons, ketch rigged, carrying square sails on the mainmast. She had been built by Phineas Pett at Greenwich for Charles II, and was called after the king's pet name for the Duchess of Portsmouth. The hull was profusely gilded, with a mass of carving at bow and stern, and a broadside of half a dozen guns was meant only for ceremonial purposes. After commanding a ship of war such a vessel must have seemed like a toy, but the appointment was a mark of favour, and given to a discreet and trustworthy officer. Richard took the Prince and Princess of Brunswick to and from the Continent on a number of occasions, and in the summer of 1765 brought back the Duke of York from Holland. He was now moving in exalted social circles, but there can be little doubt that he was relieved to be appointed to a seagoing command again. This was in 1766 when he was made Commander-in-Chief Mediterranean, wearing his flag aboard H.M.S. "Jersey". It is a measure of the naval retrenchment that in spite of Richard's exalted position, the "Jersey" was only a fourth rate of 50 guns, the remaining ten ships in his squadron being fifth and sixth rates.

Richard had not served in the Mediterranean since his far off days as a midshipman aboard H.M.S. "Canterbury". Now, aged fifty, he found himself called on to exercise considerable tact and diplomatic skills. These were particularly needed in dealing with those important but unreliable allies of England, the Dey of Algiers and the Emperor of Morocco. The rulers of the Barbary States were supported by Britain as a counter to the power of Spain and France. Nevertheless they frequently made things difficult by their attacks on the merchant ships of Mediterranean powers, even in times of peace. They behaved like pirates, robbing the ships of their cargoes, and taking their crews as slaves. They also made exorbitant demands on their ally, for such items as guns and gunpowder, or ships stores, - compasses, anchors and the like. At times, if their requests for finance were not met, they would use it as an excuse to attack British ships also. Richard repeatedly made visits to Tetuan and Algiers, acting as King George III's plenipotentiary. He seems to have been reasonably successful in these diplomatic moves, although at other times we find him having to arrange for his squadron to convoy British merchantmen past the Barbary coasts.

Among other duties Richard was called on to convey many notables about the Mediterranean. He carried Admiral Sir George Pocock to Villefranche, and then picked up the Prince of Brunswick at Marseilles. He gives a passage to his old friend Admiral Augustus Keppel, and the Marchioness of Tavistock, from Portugal to Italy. While lying in Port Mahon, H.M.S. "Jersey" had to be painted throughout because the Emperor of Germany expressed a desire to look over an English man-of-war. It was worlds away from Richard's life in the late campaign. In 1767 a less pleasant duty required him to wait once again on the Duke of York at Monaco. The prince had died there and Richard was required to despatch his remains to Portsmouth. (Among other details a midshipman and four seamen were given the task of going ashore to collect H.R.H.'s bowels!)

In addition to all this socialising went the endless familiar routine of looking after ships and men. In one particular at least this had become easier. Ships in tropical seas were now being fitted under water with thin sheets of copper as a protection against fouling. One of the ships in Richard's squadron was H.M.S. "Alarm", a 32 gun frigate under the command of Captain John Jervis. She was the first ship to have been thus fitted in 1761, and the experiment had proved so successful that gradually all other warships would be so treated. Richard notes that now the ships only needed to be cleaned under water once a year.

After three years in the Mediterranean H.M.S. "Jersey" was recalled to England. Before he left Richard had a young officer Thomas Davey, who had just passed for lieutenant, transferred to his own ship. It was a significant act, for Davey was his sister Mary's son, and he was a young man who would figure increasingly in Richard's personal life. A few years later Richard used his position to promote Lieutenant Davey to the command of a sloop, H.M.S. "Diligence". Davey was then aged twenty-six, and in peace time such a move was a great step forward.

Soon after his return to England, Richard was himself promoted as Rear Admiral of the Blue, in charge of the Channel Squadron, and back once more in Plymouth. This would be the peak of his naval career, and his seagoing days were almost over, being restricted to a short cruise to the westward each summer. He lived ashore most of the time in Plymouth Dock although his flag was carried aboard a succession of ships in the Hamoaze, ships with famous names such as "Trident", "Ocean", "Torbay" and "Albion". His letters and orders deal with the fitting out and sailing of vessels, but even more with the men that served in them. There was much action against smugglers and deserters, and much to do with the securing of people for the fleet.

Meanwhile a new war was brewing against a totally unexpected enemy. The conquest of Canada, and the removal of the danger from the French had led to a widening rift between the American colonists and the British government. As early as 1765 Parliament had passed the Stamp Act, which very reasonably required the colonists to pay for their own defence. But the colonists equally reasonably claimed that there should be no taxation without representation. Incidents followed one upon the other: the Boston massacre, the Boston tea party, and then actual warfare at Lexington and Bunker Hill in 1775.

Richard must have observed the growth of hostilities with astonishment. He had known America as a string of separate colonies with their own laws and their own governors, colonies much given to quarrelling among themselves over such matters as state borders, or fishing rights. He can never have visualised that they would make common cause against the mother country. In Plymouth, the nearest naval base to the Americas, there seemed little sense of urgency at first.

Ships sailed to and from the West Indies or Boston or Nova Scotia, but there is no indication of extensive preparation for war.

The truth is that Richard Spry was a sick man, nearing the end of his service, and no longer the man to deal with a crisis. He spent several months at Bath, taking the waters against the stomach complaint which had plagued his last years at sea. Moreover, the Navy was also suffering from the political intrigues of peace time. The Earl of Sandwich had been First Lord of the Admiralty since 1771, and money that should have been spent on ships went on jobbery and corruption. It was a situation remarkably like that which had existed when Richard first joined the service, and one which any individual would find difficult to fight against. While British sea power waned, across the Channel Choiseul was rebuilding the French Navy against the time when it might be revenged for the defeats of the last war.

One of Richard's last voyages took him in H.M.S. "Ocean" to Portsmouth in the summer of 1773, where he commanded the fleet for a review by King George III. There, on the deck of his flagship the king knighted him as a "knight banneret". This was an old honour, usually given to those who had distinguished themselves on the field of battle, and was a fitting reward for an ageing warrior.

In the following spring his Rear Admiral's flag was hauled down for the last time, and his active service was over. One of his last orders show something of the more humane side of his old age. A seaman aboard H.M.S. "Torbay", one J. McDonald, had committed the crime of striking a junior officer. For this he was court-martialled and sentenced to a flogging of 500 lashes round the fleet. It was a savage sentence that was almost the equivalent of a death sentence. McDonald withstood 350 lashes before he collapsed. When a surgeon reported that any further punishment would endanger his life, the Admiral ordered an end to it and directed that the "poor fellow" should be released from the Navy.

When Richard left the service and went back to St. Anthony he was aged sixty, and might have expected a few years of happy retirement. There was plenty to do. The old house and church had been much neglected, and as a rich man he could see to their restoration. There was still fishing in Percuil river, and shooting in the woods along the shore. But in little more than a year he died, leaving his wealth and lands and family name to his nephew Captain Thomas Davey. They buried him in the churchyard, and Captain Davey put up a handsome marble memorial in the church. This sets out briefly some of his achievements, but says little of the quality of the man.

Robert Louis Stevenson in his essay "The English Admirals" writes that admirals and prize fighters are admired by all classes of society. "Their sayings and doings stir English blood like the sound of a trumpet: and if the Indian Empire, the trade of London, and all the outward and visible ensigns of our greatness should pass away, we should still leave behind us a durable monument of what we were, in the sayings and doings of the English Admirals."

Stevenson was writing in the nineteenth century, and it is doubtful whether such an observation would meet with general approval today. Only the names of a few admirals such as Nelson, Drake, Benbow are widely known. There are countless others, fine seamen like Saunders, Hughes, Warren, Boscawen, who are rarely given due recognition for their courage and devotion. They probably did not expect it, for they gave honourable service and fought against men and the elements as a matter of duty. Among them, perhaps as a lesser star, we should surely count Admiral Richard Spry.

# APPENDICES

## APPENDIX I

### HIS MAJESTY'S BOMB "COMET"

The bomb-sloop "Comet", which Richard Spry took under his command in September 1744, might at a later date have been called a bomb-ketch. In the 18th century nautical terminology was more fluid than it is today[1]. The "Comet" was a single decked vessel with two masts, both crossing square yards. A "bomb" was specially built to mount heavy brass mortars on her deck. In order to make room for these the foremast was set well back from the bow, giving the vessel the ungainly appearance of a three masted ship that had lost her forward mast. It was this that first led Captain Le Gras of "La Brador" to engage.

A sunken well was constructed forward of each mast to take the mortars. Here the deck was strengthened underneath with additional heavy wooden beams, stiffened at their ends with iron knees.

The two 10″ mortars rested in their wells on trunnions, and together weighed several tons. There was no proper system of recoil, but they were held in place by heavy blocks and tackles, and the space below the deck at that point stuffed with old rope to reduce the shock of firing.

Mortars were weapons of tremendous destructive power, particularly against fortifications. They were useless against a moving target. When an attack was made against a fortress from the sea, the bomb vessel was anchored as close inshore as might be thought prudent, and lobbed her shot into the defences. "Bombs" had been developed by the French at the end of the seventeenth century, and Admiral Vernon used them with great effect in his attack on Porto Bello in 1740, where Captain Charles Knowles, Richard Spry's patron, had been in charge of them. The year before Richard had command of her, the "Comet" took part in an action at La Guayra on the Spanish American mainland.

Because of their general unhandiness, and the devastating effect of noise and blast when the mortars were fired, few men welcomed service in a bomb vessel. Yet it is apparent that Richard Spry grew very fond of his first command. True she was small and rather squat, being only 92 feet long to 26 feet beam, and her trim was a little down by the head. But she was a new vessel, having been built on the Thames, at Rotherhithe in 1742, and he had shown that properly handled she could take on an adversary of twice her size.

---

[1] She would probably be called a brig now.

171

## APPENDIX II

### SHIPS AND CAPTAINS

**Anson's Fleet. April 1747**

Namur, (Boscawen). Eagle, (Rodney). Falkland, (Borradall). Hampton Court, (Mostyn). Prince George, (Vice-Admiral Anson, Brett). Prince Frederick (Norris). Nottingham, (Saumarez). Centurion, (Dennis). Defiance, (Grenville). Lyon, (Scott). Bristol, (Montagu). Pembroke, (Fincher). Devonshire, (Rear Admiral Warren, West). Monmouth, (Harrison). Chester (Spry). Windsor, (Hanway). Princess Louisa, (Watson). Kent (Fox).

There were two fire-ships, and several sloops.

**Ships on the American Coast under Commodore R. Spry.    October 1755**

Fougueux, (Spry). Centurion, (Mantell). Litchfield, (Barton). Norwich, (Barrington). Success, (Rous). Vulture, (Scaife). Jamaica, (Hood). Syren, (Proby). Baltimore, (Owen). Garland, (Arbuthnot). Nightingale, (Digg). Mermaid, (Shirley). Hornet, (Salt). Otter, (Innes).

**Fleet off Louisbourg under Vice Admiral Holburne.    September 1757**

Kingston, (Parry). Tilbury, (Barnesley). Grafton, (Commodore Holmes, Cornwall). Captain, (Rear Admiral Hardy, Amherst). Somerset, (Hughes). Terrible, (Collins). Newark, (Vice Admiral F. Holburne, W. Holburne). Orford, (Spry). Northumberland, (Colville). Bedford, (Fawkes). Sunderland, (McKenzie). Centurion, (Mantell). Invincible, (Bentley). Defiance, (Beard). Nassau, (Sawyer). Windsor, (Faulkner). Devonshire, (Gordon). Prince Frederick, (Harman). Nottingham, (Marshall). Eagle, (Palliser). There were also seven sloops:- Hawke, Lightning, Speedwell, Hunter, Ferret, Furnace, Gibraltar's Prize.

**Spry's Squadron off Ushant 1761.**

Orford, (Spry). Edgar, (Drake). Hampton Court, (Scrope). Princess Amelie, (Montagu). Royal William, (Pigot). Chichester, (Elliot). Prince Frederick, (Maplesden). Rippon, (Jekyll). Essex, (Schomberg). Burford, (Gambier). Thames, (Elliot). There were also four frigates:- Aeolus, Niger, Arethusa, Aquilon.

## APPENDIX III

### GLOSSARY

**Admiral of the Blue.** Admirals were promoted in three grades, - Admiral, Vice-Admiral, and Rear-Admiral, in that order of seniority. Fleets were also divided, into three squadrons, Red, White or Blue, and the ships flew the appropriate ensign at their stern. Something of that old tradition has been preserved today in that naval vessels wear the white ensign, naval reserve vessels the blue, and merchant ships the red.

**Bilge.** The rounded part of the hull where the side planking joins the bottom. Inside the hull, the part where water would drain.

**Brig.** A two masted sailing vessel, square rigged on both masts.

**Brought-to.** The way of the ship checked by bringing her into the wind.

**Bowline.** A line taken to the bow to haul the weather side of a square sail forward.

**Bulkhead.** A partition dividing one part of a ship from another.

**Cable.** 1) Anchor rope. 2) A distance of $\frac{1}{10}$ of a nautical mile, or about 200 yards.

**Careen.** Haul a vessel over on to her side so that work might be carried out on the bottom.

**Cat.** Type of small merchant vessel.

**Cutter.** A ship's boat which could be rowed or sailed. The name was also used to describe a single masted vessel used in the service to pursue smugglers.

**Flogging around the fleet.** A particularly severe punishment by which the offender was rowed from ship to ship in harbour, and flogged by the entry port of each one. The punishment could run to five hundred lashes, and very few men could survive the ordeal.

**Grego.** A rough jacket or watch coat, fitted with a hood.

**Heave-to.** Trim the sails so that the vessel lies head to wind, almost stopped.

**Jury rig.** Temporary repair of a damaged mast or rudder, so that the vessel may continue to sail.

**Lee.** Shelter from the wind.

**Lee side.** The side of the ship away from the wind.

**Lee Shore.** The shore on the lee side of the ship, towards which the wind would be blowing.

**Pendant (or Pennant).** A triangular shaped flag.

**Purser.** The warrant officer responsible for provisions.

**Quarter-deck.** The afterdeck of a warship which contained the officers quarters. On bigger vessels it was partly covered by the poop.

**Rate.** Applied to naval vessels it was an indication of their size. In Spry's day it accorded with the number of guns a vessel carried. Allowing for minor variations, a first rate carried 100 guns, a second rate about 90 - 100, a third rate about 65 - 85. All of these were ships of the line. Fourth rates carried 50 - 60 guns and were not considered "battle ships", although they often fought in the line of battle. The terms fifth rate (30 - 45 guns) and sixth rate (20 - 30 guns) were applied to small single decked vessels such as frigates. Smaller vessels still, were generally termed sloops. First and second rates were normally three deckers, third and fourth were two deckers.

**Rig.** Properly speaking a ship was a three masted vessel, square rigged on all masts.

A ship rigged vessel of about 1750

1) Spritsail. 2) Jib. 3) Fore topmast staysail. 4) Foresail. 5) Fore topsail. 6) Fore topgallant. 7) Main topmast staysail. 8) Mainsail. 9) Main topsail. 10) Main topgallant. 11) Mizzen topsail. 12) Mizzen.

**Slops.** Supply of clothing in the care of the purser, bought for the ship and sold to the crew.

**Sloop.** In Spry's time the name was applied to a small vessel used for general work, rather than to a particular rig. The bomb-sloop "Comet" was rigged as a brig, but other sloops might well be ship rigged.

**Sprung.** When applied to a mast or spar it meant one that had been cracked.

**Tacking.** 1) Changing direction by turning into the wind. 2) Making progress by sailing to windward, - also referred to as beating.

**Wale.** A thick strake of planking. The gunwale in a small boat was the top planking.

## ACKNOWLEDGEMENTS

I have to thank the following for their considerable help.

Mr. Kingsley Cruise, Major and Mrs. N.S. Grant-Dalton, Mr. Norman Hannan, the Staffs of the Cornwall County Records Office, and the Royal Institution of Cornwall, the Librarians of the National Maritime Museum, the Committees of the Quiller Couch Memorial Fund.

## BIBLIOGRAPHY

Log Books, Order Books, Journals and Muster Books of
Captain R. Spry, R.N.
The Influence of Sea Power upon History. A.T. Mahan.
The Naval Side of British History. G. Callender.
England in the Seven Years War. J. Corbett.
The Navy in the War of 1739-48. H.W. Richmond.
Sea Life in Nelson's Time. J. Masefield.
Roderick Random. A. Smollet.
Louisbourg from its Foundation to its Fall. J.S. McLennan.
Medecine and the Navy. J.J. Keevil.
The Dictionary of National Biography.

# INDEX OF PEOPLE, PLACES, SHIPS

## PEOPLE

Wallis, Capt. 114
Walpole, R. 110
Ward, Capt. 47
Warren, Adm. P.  2, 35, 36, 47, 48, 49,
    54, 56, 59, 60, 65, 72, 76, 97
Washington, Gen. G. 107
Watson, Adm. C. 102

Willard, Capt. 40
Wolfe, Gen. J. 133, 134, 135, 137,
    138, 143, 146

Yeo, Capt. J. 16
Yorke, Col. 109

## PLACES

Acadia 57, 118
America 98, 100, 104, 109
Annapolis Royal 57, 58, 59, 60, 65, 119
Antigua 7, 41, 42, 47

Beausejour 104, 115
Belle Isle (France) 156, 162
Biscay 33, 64, 76, 78, 84, 153
Brest 59, 64, 109, 132, 150, 154, 157,
    159, 160
Bohortha 9
Boston (Mass.) 5, 37, 38, 39, 47, 48,
    56, 57, 59, 119, 123, 168

Cadiz 31
Canada 49, 121, 129, 133, 134, 138,
    150
Cape Breton 48, 49, 57, 58, 64, 112,
    124, 128, 138
Cape Town 85
Cape Verde 85
Carrickfergus 100, 152
Charleston 46, 47, 123
Chebucto (Halifax) 60, 62, 65, 104
Cork 101, 128
Cuddalore 87, 95

Deal 71, 72, 80
Downs, The 27, 71, 79
Dunkirk 71

Falmouth 11, 12, 15
Fort Cumberland 124
Fort Dusquesne 107, 108, 115, 134,
    136
Fort Monckton 124
Fort Niagara 115, 120

Fort St. David 87, 88, 92
France 48, 49, 75
Fundy, Bay of 57, 104, 119, 121

Gaspe, Bay of 125
Gerrans 10, 97, 99, 103
Gibraltar 30, 31, 150
Goodwins 79
Guernsey 99, 102

Halifax (Nova Scotia) 104, 112, 115,
    121, 125, 128, 134
Hamoaze 18, 19, 21, 25
Hampton Roads 104
Havana 42, 43, 44, 46, 47, 90, 102,
    156

Ireland 44, 101

Kinsale 101, 153

Lisbon 27, 29
London 71
Louisbourg 47, 48, 50, 54, 58, 89, 112,
    122, 124, 127, 128, 129, 134, 136
Lorient 50
Louisiana 119

Madame, Isle 143
Madeira 85
Manila 164
Martinique 36, 160
Mauritius 87
Mediterranean 30, 164, 168
Minorca 30, 127, 133
Montreal 57, 100, 134
Morro Castle 43, 45

## SHIPS (all H.M.S. unless otherwise specified)

*Other titles available from*

# DYLLANSOW TRURAN

**CORNISH BEDSIDE BOOK NO. 1.**
### John Keast
Place-names, customs, dialects, remedies and recipes are nicely balanced by short essays and stories by early travellers, historical events and extracts from diaries. A throughly entertaining book.
*Card Covers* 9506431 8 1

**VISITORS TO CORNWALL**
### Ida Procter
As J.C. Trewin says in his Introduction – "Ida Procter can recreate her guests most surely... Everyone is here; Francis Kilvert for example, Ceila Fiennes is here – at St. Austell. Nearly two centuries later the young Beatrix Potter was arriving by train at Falmouth.

It is an enchanting book."

*Paperback* 0 907566 27 8

**HOW LONG IS FOREVER** *Memories of a Cornish Maid*
### Ethelwyn Watts
Born in the changing years of the decade that followed the First World War, the author describes her home parish as "perhaps the most Cornish part of Cornwall" and she paints a word picture of a magical land.

*Card Covers* 0 907566 30 . 8
*Hardback* 0 907566 89 8

# A HISTORY OF SOUTH CROFTY MINE
J. Allen Buckley

The history of this Queen of Cornish Mines, told by a working miner extraordinary. This book with photographs, illustrations and maps gives a detailed history of 300 years of working the property, lode by lode and level by level.

*Hard Covers* 0 907566 17 0

# ST. IVES MINING DISTRICT – Vol. I
Cyril Noall

In this book the whole fascinating story of mining around St. Ives is related with a wealth of detail and illustrations with numerous photographs, sections and plans. The Author, historian and Bard of the Cornish Gorsedd has already written many learned histories of Cornish mines, customs and events.

*Paper Back* 0 907566 33 2

# THE HISTORY OF THE CORNISH COPPER COMPANY
W.H. Pascoe

This book describes the History of an important undertaking in West Cornwall throughout the years of Britain's Industrial Revolution. It is the story of the only successful copper smelting firm in the whole of Cornwall, a firm also in the forefront of the development of the internationally famous Cornish Steam Engine.

*Paper Back* 0 907566 35 9

# THE KING OF MID-CORNWALL
*The Life of Joseph Thomas Treffry*
John Keast

Joseph Thomas Treffry (1792–1890) has been aptly described as "A captain of industry, master of his own economic fate, an assertive individualist soul who pioneered in the development of transportation to facilitate the exploitation of his mines and the marketing of the ores they produced!

*Paper Back* 0 907566 29 4
*Hard Back* 0 907566 19 7

## KERNEWEK MAR PLEK – Second Course
### Crysten Fudge

9506431 5 7

Cassettes are available to convert this series into a home tuition course for students of all ages.

## CORNISH SIMPLIFIED
### Caradar (A.S.D. Smith)
### Edited by Talek (E.G.R. Hooper)

Still the most complete reference book of Cornish grammar.

0 907566 09

## THE LIFE OF CORNISH
### Crysten Fudge

The story of our language to the 17th Century. An immensely scholarly and readable work. Attractively illustrated. A fascinating story told with the insight and understanding of a foremost Celtic scholar.

*Card Cover* 0 907566 20 0

## CORNISH NAMES FOR CORNISH HOMES
### Crysten Fudge, M.A.

A name-it-in-Cornish handbook, delightfully illustrated by Laura Rowe.

9506431 0 6

## NAMES FOR THE CORNISH

300 Christian names for your children – all of them Cornish. With derivations and translations.

0 907566 03  0

## A HANDBOOK OF CORNISH SURNAMES
### G. Pawley White

Dr. A.L. Rowse points out in his foreword that the study of Cornish surnames is an essential work in the elucidation of the distant Cornish identity.

9506431 9 X

**THE BOUNCING HILLS** *Dialect Tales and Light Verse*
Jack Clemo
Jack Clemo says "I contributed many dialect tales to Cornish Almanacks before the war capturing the lighter side of Clay country village life as it was 50 years ago. I have chosen eight of these stories, and have added a selection of my comic verse (not in dialect, but with a Cornish flavour). There are about 20 short poems, mostly written for or about children".

This is a book from a Cornish literary giant shedding a new light on Cornwall's own blind poet.

*Card Covers* 0 907566 38 3
*Hard Covers* 0 907566 39 1

**THE HISTORY OF FALMOUTH**
Dr. James Whetter
The author's considerable knowledge of life in the 17th Century Cornwall provides much new information about the origins of the old town – its growth over three and a half centuries and its social, cultural and religious history.

*Card Covers* 0 907566 02 2

**CARN BREA**
Michael Tangye
A book on Redruth, Illogan and Camborne's dominating feature.

Michael Tangye's expert account will meet the needs of students of all ages and all of those who are curious about 'the Carn'. Illustrated by the author.

*Card Covers* 0 907566 11 1

**CORNISH EPITAPHS Vol. I.**
John Keast
Records, humour, pathos AND sermons in stone! Beautifully illustrated with photographs, line-drawings, etc. This is volume one of a two-volume work.

*Card Covers* 0 907566 15 4

## THE LIFE OF PASSMORE EDWARDS
### R.S. Best
*(With an essay on the life of Sylvanus Trevail
by Peter Laws)*
Rising from rags to riches, he endowed nearly 70 institutions –
libraries, art galleries, hospitals, museums and an orphanage etc.
throughout Britain between the years of 1890 and 1904. The first
substantial biography of the great Cornish Benefactor.
*Card Covers* 0 907566 18 9

## THE SAINTS OF CORNWALL
### Catherine Rachel John
A comprehensive account of the many saints of Cornwall –
dedications ranging from early Celtic to modern times. Miss John
has built on the researches of her father, (Donald Attwater) Canon
Doble, and others. Illustrated with 40 photos and line-drawings.
*Linen Covers* 0 907566 14 6

## MEMORIES OF OLD PENRYN
### Florence Rapson
(Edited by Rita Tregellas Pope)
A picture of a way of life of which only nostalgic memories
remain.

0 907566 42 1

## KERNEWEK MAR PLEK!
The newest course in Cornish that has already revolutionised
Cornish Language teaching.

### KERNEWEK MAR PLEK – First Course
#### Crysten Fudge and Graham Sandercock

9506431 2 2